THE ITALIAN COOKBOOK

2022

BEST AND AUTHENTIC REGIONAL RECIPES MADE EASY

LIA AMATI

BUON

APPETITO!!!

TABLE OF CONTENTS

Ziti with Spinach and Ricotta 9

Rigatoni with Four Cheeses 11

Linguine with Creamy Nut Sauce 13

Bow Ties with Amaretti 15

Spaghetti with Fried Eggs, Salerno Style 17

Tagliarini Soufflé 20

Spaghetti, Charcoal Burner's Style 24

Bucatini with Tomatoes, Pancetta, and Hot Pepper 26

Penne with Pancetta, Pecorino, and Black Pepper 29

Penne with Pork and Cauliflower 32

Spaghetti with Vodka Sauce 35

Bow Ties with Asparagus, Cream, and Prosciutto 37

"Dragged" Penne with Meat Sauce 39

Spaghetti, Caruso Style 42

Penne with Beans and Pancetta 44

Pasta with Chickpeas 47

Rigatoni Rigoletto 49

Anna's Fried Spaghetti 52

Eggplant Pasta Timbale 55

Baked Ziti 59

Sicilian Baked Pasta 61

Sophia Loren's Baked Pasta 65

Linguine with Clam Sauce 67

Tuscan Spaghetti with Clams 70

Linguine with Anchovies and Spicy Tomato Sauce 73

Linguine with Crab and Little Tomatoes 75

Linguine with Mixed Seafood Sauce 77

Thin Spaghetti with Bottarga 80

Venetian Whole-Wheat Spaghetti in Anchovy Sauce 82

Capri-Style Spaghetti 84

Linguine with Shrimp, Venetian Style 86

Pasta with Sardines and Fennel 88

Penne with Zucchini, Swordfish, and Herbs 91

Christmas Eve Spaghetti with Baccala 94

Linguine with Tuna Pesto 97

Cold Pasta with Vegetable Confetti and Seafood 99

Fresh Egg Pasta 102

Fettuccine with Butter and Parmigiano 111

Fettuccine with Butter and Cheese 113

Summer Fruit Torte 116

Autumn Fruit Torte 118

Polenta and Pear Cake 120

Ricotta Cheesecake ... 123

Sicilian Ricotta Cake ... 125

Ricotta Crumb Cake ... 128

Stuffed Rice Timbale ... 131

Rice and Beans, Veneto Style ... 138

Sardinian Sausage Rice ... 140

Polenta ... 142

Polenta with Cream ... 144

Polenta with Ragù ... 145

Polenta Crostini, Three Ways ... 146

Polenta Sandwiches ... 149

Polenta with Three Cheeses ... 151

Polenta with Gorgonzola and Mascarpone ... 153

Mushroom Polenta ... 155

Buckwheat and Cornmeal Polenta ... 157

Baked Polenta with Cheese ... 159

Baked Polenta with Sausage Ragù ... 161

Polenta "in Chains" ... 163

Farro Salad ... 165

Farro, Amatrice Style ... 168

Farro, Tomatoes, and Cheese ... 170

Shrimp and Barley Orzotto ... 172

Barley and Vegetable Orzotto 174

Prosciutto and Eggs 176

Baked Asparagus with Eggs 179

Eggs in Purgatory 181

Eggs in Tomato Sauce, Marches Style 183

Piedmontese-Style Eggs 185

Eggs Florentine 187

Baked Eggs with Potatoes and Cheese 189

Peppers and Eggs 191

Potatoes and Eggs 193

Mushroom and Egg Scramble 196

Onion and Arugula Frittata 198

Zucchini and Basil Frittata 201

Hundred-Herb Frittata 203

Spinach Frittata 205

Mushroom and Fontina Frittata 208

Neapolitan Spaghetti Frittata 210

Pasta Frittata 212

Little Omelets 214

Ricotta and Zucchini Flower Frittata 216

Omelet Strips in Tomato Sauce 218

Ziti with Spinach and Ricotta

Ziti con Spinaci e Ricotta

Makes 4 to 6 servings

Spinach, ricotta, and Parmigiano-Reggiano are a typical stuffing for ravioli in Emilia-Romagna and many other regions. In this recipe, the filling for fresh pasta becomes the sauce for dried pasta. The flavors are similar, but the method is much easier for every day. Chopped cooked broccoli can stand in for the spinach if you like.

1½ pounds spinach, tough stems removed

4 tablespoons unsalted butter

1 medium onion, finely chopped

Salt

1 pound ziti or penne

1 cup whole or part-skim ricotta, at room temperature

½ cup freshly grated Parmigiano-Reggiano

Freshly ground black pepper

1. Put the spinach in a large pot over medium heat with $1/4$ cup water. Cover and cook for 2 to 3 minutes or until wilted and tender. Drain and cool. Wrap the spinach in a lint-free cloth and squeeze out as much water as possible. Finely chop the spinach.

2. In a large saucepan, melt the butter over medium-low heat. Add the onion and cook until tender and golden, about 10 minutes. Add the chopped spinach and cook, stirring, until the spinach is heated through, 3 to 4 minutes. Add salt to taste

3. Bring at least 4 quarts of water to a boil in a large pot. Add 2 tablespoons of salt, then the pasta. Stir well. Cook over high heat, stirring frequently, until the pasta is al dente, tender yet still firm to the bite. Drain the pasta, reserving some of the cooking water.

4. In a large heated serving bowl, toss the pasta with the spinach, ricotta, and cheese. Add a little of the cooking water if the pasta seems dry. Sprinkle with freshly ground black pepper and serve immediately.

Rigatoni with Four Cheeses

Rigatoni ai Quattro Formaggi

Makes 4 to 6 servings

The four cheeses suggested below are just a suggestion. Use whatever you have on hand, even pieces that are a little dried out are fine when grated. I can't think of any cheese that does not go well with pasta. I have eaten versions of this pasta in Rome, Tuscany, and Naples, and I suspect it is the kind of thing that cooks throw together whenever they have small amounts of a variety of cheeses.

1 pound rigatoni, ziti, or fusilli

Salt

6 tablespoons unsalted butter, melted

½ cup shredded Fontina Valle d'Aosta

½ cup shredded fresh mozzarella

½ cup shredded Gruyere or Emmenthal

¾ cup freshly grated Parmigiano-Reggiano

Freshly ground black pepper

1. Bring at least 4 quarts of water to a boil in a large pot. Add 2 tablespoons of salt, then the pasta. Stir well. Cook over high heat, stirring frequently, until the pasta is al dente, tender but still firm to the bite. Drain the pasta, reserving some of the cooking water.

2. In a large heated serving bowl, toss the pasta with the butter. Add the cheeses and a couple of tablespoons of the pasta water. Toss until the cheese is melted. Sprinkle with black pepper and serve immediately.

Linguine with Creamy Nut Sauce

Linguine con Salsa di Noci

Makes 4 to 6 servings

My friend Pauline Wasserman came across this recipe while traveling in Piedmont and gave it to me some years ago. The nuts give the pasta a rich flavor, while the ricotta keeps it creamy and moist. I serve it with dolcetto, a light, dry red wine from Piedmont.

½ cup walnuts

2 tablespoons pine nuts

4 tablespoons unsalted butter

1 small garlic clove, very finely chopped

1 tablespoon chopped fresh flat-leaf parsley

¼ cup whole or part-skim ricotta, mascarpone, or heavy cream

Salt

1 pound linguine

½ cup freshly grated Parmigiano-Reggiano

1. Place the walnuts and pine nuts in a food processor or blender. Grind the nuts just until fine. (Don't overprocess into a paste.)

2. In a medium skillet, melt the butter over medium heat. Add the garlic and parsley and cook 1 minute. Stir in the ground nuts and ricotta. Stir to blend and heat through.

3. Meanwhile, bring about 4 quarts of water to a boil in a large pot. Add 2 tablespoons of salt, then the pasta, gently pushing it down until the pasta is completely covered with water. Stir well. Cook, stirring often, until the pasta is al dente, tender yet still firm to the bite. Set aside some of the cooking water. Drain the pasta.

4. In a large heated serving bowl, toss the pasta with the sauce and grated cheese. Add a little of the cooking water if the pasta seems dry. Serve immediately.

Bow Ties with Amaretti

Farfalle con gli Amaretti

Makes 4 to 6 servings

One of the specialties of Lombardy is fresh egg pasta stuffed with winter squash and crushed amaretti, *crunchy almond cookies ([Winter Squash Ravioli with Butter and Almonds]()). Bathed in melted butter and sprinkled with salty and nutty Parmigiano, the combination of flavors is most unusual and unforgettable. The waiter at a little trattoria in Cremona told me that this simple recipe made with dried pasta was inspired by that elaborate dish.*

If your raisins are on the dry side, plump them by dropping them into the boiling pasta water just before draining.

Salt

1 pound farfalle

1 stick unsalted butter, melted

12 to 16 amaretti cookies, crushed (about $\frac{1}{2}$ cup crumbs)

$\frac{1}{3}$ cup golden raisins

1 cup grated Parmigiano-Reggiano

1. Bring at least 4 quarts of water to a boil in a large pot. Add 2 tablespoons of salt, then the pasta. Stir well. Cook over high heat, stirring frequently, until the pasta is al dente, tender yet still firm to the bite. Set aside some of the cooking water. Drain the pasta.

2. Place the butter in a large warm serving bowl. Add the pasta and toss it with the cookie crumbs and raisins. Add the cheese and toss again. Add a little of the cooking water if the pasta seems dry. Serve hot.

Spaghetti with Fried Eggs, Salerno Style

Spaghetti con l'Uuovo Fritto alla Salernitana

Makes 2 servings

Though I had heard about this recipe from the Naples area, I never tried making it until one day when I thought I had nothing in the house to cook for myself and my husband. It is simple and comforting and could even be served for brunch. The eggs should be cooked until the whites are set but the yolks are still soft. The ingredients for this recipe will serve two, but you can double or triple them as needed.

4 ounces spaghetti or linguine

Salt

2 tablespoons olive oil

4 eggs

½ cup freshly grated Pecorino Romano

Freshly ground black pepper

1. **Bring at least 4 quarts of water to a boil in a large pot. Add 2 tablespoons of the salt, then the pasta, gently pushing it down

until the pasta is completely covered with water. Stir well. Cook over high heat, stirring frequently.

2. Heat the oil in a large skillet over medium heat. Add the eggs, sprinkling them with salt and pepper. Cook until the whites are just set and the yolks are still soft.

3. Drain the pasta, reserving some of the cooking water. Toss the pasta with the cheese and 2 to 3 tablespoons of the water.

4. Divide the pasta between 2 serving dishes. Top each with two eggs and serve immediately.

Tagliarini Soufflé

Soufflé di Tagliarini

Makes 6 servings

Some recipes reach my kitchen in a roundabout way. My friend Arthur Schwartz shared this unusual one with me. He learned it from his cooking school partner, Baronessa Cecilia Bellelli Baratta, who in turn learned it from her mother, Elvira. The Baratta family lives in Battipaglia, in the province of Salerno, where Cecilia's father was in the tomato packing business. But for the duration of World War II, the family lived in Parma, where it was much safer.

Elvira (at age 91) still cooks many dishes from Parma and claims to have created the idea of a pasta soufflé while living in that region, though in fact other versions do exist. Cecilia points out that northern Italians hardly have a monopoly on egg pasta and cream sauces, no matter what the rest of us think.

What is different about this recipe is that it is made with dried egg pasta rather than fresh. Look for tagliarini, cappellini, *or* cappelli di angelo, *though ordinary thin egg noodles would work as well. The lemon flavor makes the dish seem even lighter than it is.*

Béchamel Sauce

4 tablespoons unsalted butter

4 tablespoons all-purpose flour

2 cups milk

¾ cup grated Parmigiano-Reggiano

⅛ teaspoon freshly grated nutmeg

1½ teaspoons salt

½ teaspoon freshly ground black pepper

Finely grated zest of 1 lemon

Juice of 1 lemon

4 large eggs, separated

Salt

8 ounces dried tagliarini, or another fine dried egg pasta, broken into 3-inch lengths

4 tablespoons unsalted butter

1 egg white

¼ cup plus 2 tablespoons plain dry bread crumbs

1. Prepare the sauce: Melt the butter in a small saucepan over medium heat. Stir in the flour using a whisk and let cook for 2 minutes.

2. Whisking constantly, add the milk. Bring to a simmer, stirring frequently. Remove from the heat and stir in the cheese. Allow to cool slightly before stirring in the nutmeg, salt, pepper, lemon zest, and juice.

3. Scrape the mixture into a large mixing bowl and let cool to room temperature. (Or, if you are in a hurry, cool the mixture by placing the bowl in another bowl filled with ice water.) Stir in the egg yolks, mixing thoroughly.

4. Bring about 3 quarts of water to a boil. Add 2 tablespoons of salt, then the pasta. Boil it until it is only half done. The pasta will be flexible but still hard in the center. Drain well. Transfer the pasta back to the pot it was cooked in and toss with 2 tablespoons of the remaining butter. Let the pasta cool slightly.

5. Place a rack in the center of the oven. Preheat the oven to 375°F. Using 1 tablespoon of the remaining butter, grease a 9 × 9 × 2–

inch baking dish. Sprinkle with about $1/4$ cup of the bread crumbs, coating the dish well.

6. In a large bowl with an electric mixer on medium speed, beat the egg whites with a pinch of salt until soft peaks form. Gently fold the whites into the béchamel sauce. With a rubber spatula, fold the sauce into the pasta a little at a time. Work carefully so as not to deflate the whites too much. Scrape the mixture into the prepared baking dish.

7. Sprinkle with the remaining 2 tablespoons bread crumbs. Dot with the remaining 1 tablespoon of butter.

8. Bake for 30 minutes or until the soufflé is puffed and lightly golden.

9. For maximum lightness, cut into squares and serve immediately. The soufflé will sink slightly as it cools.

Spaghetti, Charcoal Burner's Style

Spaghetti alla Carbonara

Makes 6 to 8 servings

Romans credit the hard-working charcoal delivery man as the inspiration for this quickly made pasta. They say the generous grinding of black pepper resembles specks of coal dust!

Some cooks in the United States add cream to the sauce, but this is the way it is made in Rome.

4 ounces pancetta, cut into thick slices

1 tablespoon olive oil

3 large eggs

Salt and freshly ground black pepper

1 pound spaghetti or linguine

3/4 cup freshly grated Pecorino Romano or Parmigiano-Reggiano

1. Cut the pancetta into $1/4$-inch pieces. Pour the oil into a skillet large enough to hold all of the cooked pasta. Add the pancetta.

Cook over medium heat, until the pancetta is golden around the edges, about 10 minutes. Turn off the heat.

2. In a medium bowl, beat the eggs with a generous amount of salt and pepper.

3. Bring at least 4 quarts of water to a boil in a large pot. Add 2 tablespoons of salt, then the pasta, gently pushing it down until the pasta is completely covered with water. Stir well. Cook over high heat, stirring frequently, until the pasta is al dente, tender yet still firm to the bite. Drain the pasta, reserving some of the cooking water.

4. Place the cooked pasta in the pan with the pancetta and toss well over medium heat. Add the eggs and a little of the cooking water. Toss gently until the pasta looks creamy. Sprinkle with cheese and more pepper. Toss well and serve immediately.

Bucatini with Tomatoes, Pancetta, and Hot Pepper

Bucatini all'Amatriciana

Makes 4 to 6 servings

Amatrice is the name of a town in the Abruzzo region. Many people from that area settled in Rome, and this recipe became one of the city's signature dishes. As with all traditions, everyone argues about the right way to uphold it. I once listened to a Roman call-in radio program on the subject that went on for an hour discussing the pros and cons of adding onion.

I have tried numerous versions, and this is the way I like it best. Bucatini, *a very thick spaghetti shape with a hole in the center, is traditional but hard to eat. Unlike spaghetti, linguine, and other long pasta strands, it does not twirl neatly around the fork, especially if it is cooked firm the way the Romans like it. A short thin pasta tube like penne is also good and a lot neater to eat.*

2 tablespoons olive oil

2 ounces sliced pancetta, about $1/8$ inch thick, chopped into tiny bits

1 medium onion, finely chopped

Pinch of crushed red pepper

½ cup dry white wine

1 (28-ounce) can imported Italian peeled tomatoes, drained and chopped

Salt

1 pound bucatini, perciatelli, or penne

½ cup freshly grated Pecorino Romano

1. Pour the oil into a skillet large enough to hold all of the cooked pasta. Add the pancetta, onion, and crushed red pepper. Cook, stirring occasionally, over medium heat, until the pancetta and onion are golden, about 12 minutes.

2. Add the wine and bring to a simmer.

3. Stir in the tomatoes and salt to taste. Bring the sauce to a simmer and cook, stirring occasionally, until the sauce is thickened, about 25 minutes.

4. Bring at least 4 quarts of water to a boil in a large pot. Add 2 tablespoons of salt, then the pasta. Stir well. Cook over high heat, stirring frequently, until the pasta is al dente, tender yet still

firm to the bite. Set aside some of the cooking water. Drain the pasta.

5. Pour the pasta into the pan with the sauce. Toss the pasta and sauce together over high heat about 1 minute, or until the pasta is coated. Add a little cooking water if the pasta seems dry. Remove from the heat. Add the cheese and toss well. Serve immediately.

Penne with Pancetta, Pecorino, and Black Pepper

Penne alla Gricia

Makes 4 to 6 servings

I was reminded of how good this pasta can be at New York's San Domenico Restaurant, where it was prepared for a luncheon celebrating the cooking of Rome. I had to include it in this collection.

Penne alla Gricia is a close relative, and quite possibly the forerunner, of the Bucatini all'Amatriciana at left. Traditional recipes for both have the same ingredients—salted meat, lard, and grated sheep's cheese, which were the typical flavorings for pasta before tomatoes arrived from the New World and were accepted in Italy. Pork lard adds a very good flavor, but olive oil can be substituted if you prefer.

In Rome, this is made with guanciale, *cured pork cheek. Unless you live near an Italian specialty butcher, guanciale is hard to find, but pancetta is very similar. Have the slices cut about ⅛-inch thick, if you can. To make the slices easier to chop, try freezing them briefly on a piece of wax paper.*

2 tablespoons pork lard or olive oil

4 ounces sliced guanciale or pancetta, about ⅛ inch thick, chopped into tiny bits

Salt

1 pound spaghetti

½ cup freshly grated Pecorino Romano

½ teaspoon freshly ground black pepper or more to taste

1. In a skillet large enough to hold all of the cooked pasta, heat the lard or olive oil over medium heat. Add the guanciale or pancetta, and cook, stirring frequently, 10 minutes or until crisp and golden brown.

2. Bring at least 4 quarts of water to a boil in a large pot. Add 2 tablespoons of salt, then the pasta. Stir well. Cook over high heat, stirring frequently, until the pasta is al dente, tender yet still firm to the bite. Set aside some of the cooking water. Drain the pasta.

3. Pour the pasta into the skillet and toss it with the cheese, pepper, and a couple of tablespoons of the water until the pasta is well coated. Serve immediately with more pepper, if desired.

Penne with Pork and Cauliflower

Pasta Incaciata

Makes 4 to 6 servings

My friend Carmella Ragusa showed me how to make this recipe, which she learned when visiting her family in Sicily.

2 tablespoons olive oil

2 garlic cloves, finely chopped

8 ounces ground pork

1 teaspoon fennel seeds

½ cup dry red wine

1 pound fresh plum tomatoes, peeled, seeded, and chopped, or 2 cups canned imported Italian tomatoes, drained and chopped

Salt and freshly ground black pepper

3 cups cauliflower florets

1 pound penne

About 1 cup freshly grated Pecorino Romano

1. Pour the oil into a large skillet. Add the the garlic and cook over medium heat until golden, about 2 minutes. Add the pork and fennel seeds and stir well. Cook, stirring occasionally, until the meat is browned, about 15 minutes.

2. Add the wine and simmer 3 minutes, or until most of the liquid evaporates.

3. Add the tomatoes and salt and pepper to taste. Simmer 15 minutes or until the sauce is slightly reduced.

4. Bring at least 4 quarts of water to a boil in a large pot. Add the cauliflower and 2 tablespoons of salt. Cook until the cauliflower is tender, about 10 minutes. With a slotted spoon, scoop out the cauliflower and drain well. Do not discard the water.

5. Add the cauliflower to the sauce and cook, stirring frequently and breaking up the pieces with a spoon, until the sauce is thick, about 10 minutes more.

6. Bring the water back to a boil and add the pasta. Cook, stirring frequently, until the pasta is al dente, tender yet still firm to the bite. Set aside some of the cooking water. Drain the pasta.

7. Transfer the pasta to a heated serving bowl. Toss the pasta with the sauce, thinning it if necessary with the cooking water. Add the cheese and toss well. Serve immediately.

Spaghetti with Vodka Sauce

Spaghetti alla Vodka

Makes 4 to 6 servings

According to my friend Arthur Schwartz, a cookbook author and food authority, this pasta was invented in the 1970s in Italy as part of an advertising campaign for a major vodka company. I first had it in Rome, but it seems to be more popular now in the United States than it is in Italy.

¼ cup unsalted butter

¼ cup finely chopped shallots

2 ounces sliced imported Italian prosciutto, cut into thin strips

1 (28-ounce) can imported Italian peeled tomatoes, drained and coarsely chopped

½ teaspoon crushed red pepper

Salt

½ cup heavy cream

¼ cup vodka

1 pound spaghetti or linguine

½ cup freshly grated Parmigiano-Reggiano

1. In a skillet large enough to hold all of the cooked pasta, melt the butter over medium heat. Add the shallots and cook until golden, about 2 minutes. Stir in the prosciutto and cook 1 minute.

2. Add the tomatoes, crushed red pepper, and salt to taste. Simmer 5 minutes. Stir in the cream and cook, stirring well, for 1 minute more. Add the vodka and cook 2 minutes.

3. Bring 4 quarts of water to a boil in a large pot. Add 2 tablespoons of salt, then the pasta, gently pushing it down until the pasta is completely covered with water. Cook over high heat, stirring frequently, until al dente, tender yet still firm to the bite. Set aside some of the cooking water. Drain the pasta.

4. Add the pasta to the skillet with the sauce. Toss the pasta in the sauce over high heat until it is well coated. Add a little cooking water if the sauce seems too thick. Stir in the cheese and toss again. Serve immediately.

Bow Ties with Asparagus, Cream, and Prosciutto

Farfalle con Asparagi

Makes 6 to 8 servings

This combination is perfect for a spring menu. I find the cream makes it very rich, so I tend to serve this pasta in small portions as a first course before something simple like grilled veal or chicken. I have added chopped roasted peppers to this pasta and like the combination very much.

1 pound fresh asparagus, trimmed

Salt

1 cup heavy cream

1 pound farfalle

½ cup freshly grated Parmigiano-Reggiano

2 ounces sliced imported Italian prosciutto, cut crosswise into thin strips

1. In a large skillet, bring about 2 inches of water to a boil. Add the asparagus and salt to taste. Cook until the asparagus are just tender and bend slightly when lifted from the water. The cooking time will depend on the thickness of the asparagus. Pat the asparagus dry. Cut them into bite-size pieces.

2. Bring the cream to a simmer in a small saucepan. Cook 5 minutes or until slightly thickened.

3. Bring a large pot of water to a boil. Add 2 tablespoons of salt, then the pasta. Stir well. Cook over high heat, stirring frequently, until the pasta is al dente, tender yet still firm to the bite. Set aside some of the cooking water. Drain the pasta.

4. Pour the pasta, cream, and cheese into a large serving bowl and toss well. Add a little cooking water if the sauce seems too thick. Add the asparagus and prosciutto and toss again. Serve immediately.

"Dragged" Penne with Meat Sauce

Penne Strascinate

Makes 6 servings

I first had this pasta at a little country restaurant in Tuscany, a region in which every cook has her or his own way of making it. It is called "dragged" penne because the pasta finishes cooking as it is stirred in the sauce. This infuses the pasta with the flavor of the sauce.

¼ cup olive oil

1 medium onion, finely chopped

1 medium carrot, finely chopped

1 tender celery rib, finely chopped

1 garlic clove, very finely chopped

2 tablespoons chopped fresh basil

12 ounces ground veal

½ cup dry red wine

2 cups peeled, seeded, and chopped fresh tomatoes or canned imported Italian peeled tomatoes, drained and chopped

1 cup homemade Meat Broth or Chicken Broth or store-bought beef or chicken broth

Salt and freshly ground black pepper

1 pound penne

½ cup freshly grated Pecorino Romano

½ cup freshly grated Parmigiano-Reggiano

1. Pour the oil into a skillet large enough to hold all of the cooked pasta. Add the onion, carrot, celery, garlic, and basil. Cook over medium heat until the vegetables are tender, about 10 minutes.

2. Add the veal and cook, stirring frequently to break up any lumps, about 10 minutes. Add the wine and bring to a simmer. Cook 1 minute.

3. Stir in the tomatoes, the broth, and salt and pepper to taste. Simmer on low heat 45 minutes, stirring occasionally.

4. Bring 4 quarts of water to a boil in a large pot. Add 2 tablespoons of salt, then the pasta. Stir well. Cook over high heat,

stirring frequently, until the pasta is almost tender but slightly underdone. Set aside some cooking water. Drain the pasta.

5. Add the pasta to the skillet and raise the heat to medium. Cook, stirring the pasta well, for 2 minutes, adding some of the water if necessary. Stir in the cheeses and serve immediately.

Spaghetti, Caruso Style

Spaghetti Enrico Caruso

Makes 6 servings

Enrico Caruso, the great Neapolitan tenor, loved to cook and eat. Pasta was his specialty, and this is said to have been one of his favorites.

¼ cup olive oil

¼ cup finely chopped shallots or onions

8 ounces chicken livers, trimmed and cut into bite-size pieces

1 teaspoon finely chopped rosemary

Salt and freshly ground black pepper

2 cups peeled, seeded, and chopped fresh tomatoes, or canned imported Italian peeled tomatoes, drained and chopped

1 pound spaghetti or linguine

2 tablespoons unsalted butter

½ cup freshly grated Parmigiano-Reggiano

1. Pour the oil into a skillet large enough to hold all of the pasta. Add the shallots. Cook over medium heat until tender, about 3 minutes. Add the livers, rosemary, and salt and pepper to taste. Cook 2 minutes or until the livers are no longer pink.

2. Stir in the tomatoes and bring to a simmer. Cook 20 minutes or until slightly thickened.

3. Bring 4 quarts of water to a boil in a large pot. Add 2 tablespoons of salt, then the pasta, gently pushing it down until the pasta is completely covered with water. Stir well. Cook over high heat, stirring frequently, until the pasta is al dente, tender yet still firm to the bite. Set aside some of the cooking water. Drain the pasta.

4. Add the spaghetti to the sauce and toss together 1 minute over high heat. Add a little cooking water if the sauce seems too thick. Add the butter and cheese and toss again. Serve immediately.

Penne with Beans and Pancetta

Penne e Fagioli

Makes 4 to 6 servings

Some pasta and bean recipes are thick and souplike, with equal parts beans and pasta. This Tuscan version is really pasta with a bean and tomato sauce.

2 tablespoons olive oil

2½ ounces pancetta, finely chopped

1 medium onion, finely chopped

1 large garlic clove, peeled and finely chopped

2 cups drained cooked or canned cranberry or cannellini beans

1½ pounds plum tomatoes, peeled, seeded, and chopped, or 3 cups canned imported Italian tomatoes, drained and chopped

Salt to taste

1 pound penne

Freshly ground black pepper

½ cup chopped flat-leaf parsley

½ cup freshly grated Parmigiano-Reggiano

1. Pour the oil into a large saucepan. Add the pancetta. Cook over medium heat, stirring occasionally, 10 minutes or until lightly browned. Add the onion and cook until it is tender and golden, about 10 minutes.

2. Stir in the garlic and cook 1 minute more. Add the beans, tomatoes, and salt and pepper. Cook 5 minutes.

3. Bring about 4 quarts of water to a boil in a large pot. Add 2 tablespoons of salt, then the pasta. Stir well. Cook over high heat, stirring frequently, until the pasta is al dente, tender yet still firm to the bite. Set aside some of the cooking water. Drain the pasta.

4. In a large warm serving bowl, toss the pasta with the sauce and parsley. Add a little of the cooking water, if needed. Add the cheese and toss again. Serve with freshly grated Parmigiano-Reggiano.

Pasta with Chickpeas

Pasta e Ceci

Makes 4 servings

A drizzle of extra-virgin olive oil is the perfect finishing touch for pasta with chickpeas. If you want to make it spicy, try it with some of the [Holy Oil](#).

2 tablespoons olive oil

2 ounces thick-sliced pancetta, finely chopped

1 medium onion, chopped

1 pound tomatoes, peeled, seeded, and chopped

1 tablespoon chopped fresh sage

Pinch of crushed red pepper

Salt

2 cups drained cooked or canned chickpeas

8 ounces small pasta, such as elbow or ditali

Extra-virgin olive oil

1. Pour the oil into a large saucepan. Add the pancetta and onion and cook, stirring occasionally, over medium heat, about 10 minutes or until tender and golden.

2. Add the tomatoes, $1/2$ cup water, sage, red pepper, and salt to taste. Bring to a simmer and cook 15 minutes. Add the chickpeas and cook 10 minutes more.

3. Bring about 4 quarts of water to a boil in a large pot. Stir in 2 tablespoons of salt, then the pasta. Stir well. Cook, stirring frequently, until the pasta is tender yet firm to the bite. Set aside some of the cooking water. Drain the pasta.

4. Add the pasta to the pan with the sauce. Stir well and bring to a simmer, adding some of the cooking water if needed. Serve immediately.

Rigatoni Rigoletto

Pasta al Rigoletto

Makes 6 servings

This pasta is named for Rigoletto, the tragic hero of Verdi's glorious opera. The story is set in Mantua, where this pasta is well known.

2 or 3 Italian-style pork sausages (about 12 ounces)

2 tablespoons olive oil

1 medium onion, finely chopped

2 garlic cloves, finely chopped

4 tablespoons tomato paste

2 cups water

2 cups cooked dried cranberry or cannellini beans, lightly drained

Salt and freshly ground black pepper

1 pound rigatoni

1 tablespoon unsalted butter

¼ cup finely chopped fresh basil

½ cup freshly grated Parmigiano-Reggiano

1. Remove the casings from the sausages and finely chop the meat.

2. Pour the oil into a saucepan large enough to hold all of the ingredients. Add the onion, sausage meat, and garlic. Cook over medium heat, stirring frequently, until the onions are tender and the sausage is lightly browned, about 15 minutes.

3. Add the tomato paste and water. Bring to a simmer and cook 20 minutes or until slightly thickened.

4. Add the beans and salt and pepper to taste. Cook 10 minutes, mashing some of the beans with the back of a spoon to make the sauce creamy.

5. Bring at least 4 quarts of water to a boil in a large pot. Add 2 tablespoons of salt, then the pasta. Stir well. Cook over high heat, stirring frequently, until the pasta is al dente, tender yet still firm to the bite. Set aside some of the cooking water. Drain the pasta.

6. Add the pasta to the pan with the sauce, toss together, and cook 1 minute, adding a little of the water if needed. Stir in the butter and basil. Add the cheese and toss again. Serve immediately.

Anna's Fried Spaghetti

Spaghetti Fritti alla Anna

Makes 4 servings

When my husband and I and a group of friends visited cooking school owner and teacher Anna Tasca Lanza at her family's farm and wine estate at Regaleali, Sicily, we shared numerous meals. Toward the end of our stay, we decided to make a casual lunch with whatever was in the refrigerator. While the rest of us were busy slicing bread and cheese, pouring wine, and making a salad, Anna took out some leftover spaghetti and poured it into a heavy skillet. In a few minutes, the pasta had turned into a crunchy golden cake that everyone devoured. Anna seemed surprised that we had enjoyed it so much and said it was just something that you can do with leftover pasta. My friend Judith Weber eventually got more information about how she had made it and passed the recipe along to me. This is great for a midnight supper, and it can be made with just about any type of leftover pasta, though long strands are best because they will stick together.

4 to 8 ounces cold leftover spaghetti with Sicilian Tomato Sauce or Marinara Sauce

3 tablespoons olive oil

2 tablespoons grated Pecorino Romano

1. Prepare the spaghetti with tomato sauce if necessary. Chill at least 1 hour or overnight.

2. In a large nonstick skillet, heat 2 tablespoons of the oil over medium heat. Sprinkle the oil with 1 tablespoon of the cheese and immediately add the pasta to the pan, pressing it flat with the back of a spoon. The pasta should be no more than $3/4$ inch deep.

3. Cook the pasta, flattening it occasionally against the pan, until golden brown and crisp on the bottom, about 20 minutes. Slide a thin spatula underneath the pasta occasionally to make sure that it is not sticking.

4. When the pasta is nicely browned, remove the skillet from heat. Slide a spatula under the pasta to be sure that the it is not stuck. Place a large inverted plate on top of the skillet. Protecting your hands with oven mitts, invert the skillet and plate so that the pasta cake falls out of the skillet onto the plate.

5. Add the remaining oil and cheese to the skillet. Slide the pasta cake with the crisp side up back into the pan. Cook the same way as the first side until browned and crisp, about 15 minutes more. Cut into wedges and serve hot.

Eggplant Pasta Timbale

Pasta al Timballo

Makes 6 servings

Pasta, cheeses, and meats encased in a dome of eggplant slices make a spectacular dish for a party or any special occasion. It is not difficult to make, but be very careful when unmolding the heavy timbale hot from the oven.

In Sicily, this is made with caciocavallo, *semifirm cow's milk cheese sold in a pear-shaped casing. The name means horse cheese, and why it is called that has been debated for centuries. Some historians think the cheese was originally made with mare's milk, while others say that it was once transported on horseback suspended from poles. Caciocavallo is similar to provolone, which can be substituted, or use Pecorino Romano.*

2 medium eggplants (about 1 pound each)

Salt

Olive oil

1 medium onion, chopped

1 garlic clove, finely chopped

8 ounces ground beef

8 ounces Italian pork sausages, skinned and chopped

2 pounds fresh tomatoes, peeled, seeded, and chopped, or 1 (28-ounce) can imported Italian peeled tomatoes, chopped

1 cup fresh or frozen peas

Freshly ground black pepper

1 pound perciatelli or bucatini

12 ounces mozzarella, chopped

1 cup freshly grated caciocavallo or Pecorino Romano

3 ounces salami, chopped

2 tablespoons chopped fresh basil

2 hard cooked eggs, sliced

1. Cut the eggplant lengthwise into $1/4$-inch thick slices. Sprinkle the slices generously with salt and place them in a colander to drain at least 30 minutes. Rinse the slices and blot dry.

2. Heat $1/4$-inch of oil in a large skillet over medium heat. Fry the slices a few at a time until lightly browned on both sides, about 5 minutes per side. Drain on paper towels.

3. Pour the oil into a large saucepan. Add the onion and garlic and cook over medium heat, stirring frequently, until the onion is softened, about 5 minutes. Add the beef and sausage meat. Cook, stirring often, until lightly browned, about 10 minutes.

4. Add the tomatoes and salt and pepper to taste. Cook on low heat 20 minutes. Add the peas and cook 10 minutes more or until the sauce is thickened.

5. Bring at least 4 quarts of water to a boil in a large pot. Add 2 tablespoons of salt, then the pasta. Stir well. Cook over high heat, stirring frequently, until the pasta is tender but still very firm. Drain the pasta and return it to the pot. Toss the pasta with the sauce. Let cool 5 minutes.

6. Line a 4-quart ovenproof bowl or baking dish with foil, pressing it smoothly against the sides. Brush the foil with olive oil. Starting in the center of the bowl, arrange half the eggplant slices, overlapping slightly against the inside and reserving a few slices for the top.

7. Add the mozzarella, grated cheese, salami, and basil to the pan with the pasta and toss well. Add half the pasta to the prepared bowl, being careful not to disturb the eggplant. Arrange the egg slices over the pasta. Top with the remaining pasta and the reserved eggplant slices. Press down lightly.

8. Place a rack in the center of the oven. Preheat the oven to 400°F. Bake 45 to 60 minutes, or until hot in the center, 140°F measured on an instant-read thermometer. (Exact baking time will depend on the diameter of the bowl.)

9. Let the timbale stand 15 minutes. Invert the bowl onto a serving plate. Remove the bowl and gently peel off the foil. Serve immediately.

Baked Ziti

Ziti al Forno

Makes 8 to 12 servings

Baked pasta dishes like this one are popular all over southern Italy. At a time when few homes had ovens, the pans of pasta would be brought to the local bakery to be cooked after the baker had finished making the day's bread.

    4 cups <u>Neapolitan Ragù</u>

Salt

1 pound ziti, penne, or rigatoni

1 pound whole or part-skim ricotta

1 cup freshly grated Pecorino Romano or Parmigiano-Reggiano cheese

12 ounces fresh mozzarella, chopped or shredded

1. Prepare the ragù, if necessary. Then, bring 4 quarts of water to a boil in a large pot. Add 2 tablespoons of salt, then the pasta. Stir well. Cook over high heat, stirring frequently, until almost tender. Drain the pasta.

2. In a large bowl, toss the pasta with 2 cups of the ragù, 1 cup of the ricotta, and half the grated cheese. Slice some of the meatballs and sausages from the ragù and stir them into the pasta. (The remaining meats can be served as a second course.)

3. Place a rack in the center of the oven. Preheat the oven to 350°F. Spread half the ziti in a 13 × 9 × 2-inch baking dish. Spread the remaining ricotta on top. Sprinkle with the mozzarella. Pour on 1 cup of the sauce. Top with the remaining ziti and another cup of sauce. Sprinkle with the remaining 1/2 cup grated cheese. Cover the dish securely with foil.

4. Bake the ziti 45 minutes. Uncover and bake 15 to 30 minutes more, or until the blade of a thin knife inserted into the center feels hot and the sauce is bubbling around the edges. Cool 15 minutes on a wire rack. Serve hot.

Sicilian Baked Pasta

Pasta al Forno alla Siciliana

Makes 12 servings

My husband's Sicilian family looked forward to eating this pasta on special occasions like Christmas and Easter. It was a specialty of his grandmother, Adele Amico, who came from Palermo.

Anellini, "little rings," are the typical pasta shape used, but they can be hard to find. Fusilli lunghi, "long fusilli," or bucatini, thick spaghetti with a hole in the center, are good substitutes. This is a perfect party dish, as it can be made in stages or completely assembled a day ahead of time, and it serves a crowd.

If you don't feel comfortable unmolding the pasta, it can be cut into squares and served directly from the pan. A 20- to 30-minute rest after baking helps the pasta to hold its shape.

Sauce

¼ cup olive oil

1 medium onion, finely chopped

2 garlic cloves, finely chopped

¼ cup tomato paste

4 (28-ounce) cans imported Italian peeled tomatoes

Salt and freshly ground black pepper

¼ cup chopped fresh basil

Filling

2 tablespoons olive oil

½ pound ground beef

½ pound ground pork

1 garlic clove, very finely chopped

Salt and freshly ground black pepper

1 cup fresh or frozen peas

2 tablespoons unsalted butter, softened

1 cup plain dry bread crumbs

2 pounds anellini or perciatelli

Salt

½ cup freshly grated Parmigiano-Reggiano

½ cup freshly grated Pecorino Romano

1 cup imported provolone, diced

1. Prepare the sauce: Pour the oil into a large saucepan. Add the onion and garlic. Cook over medium heat 10 minutes or until the onion and garlic are tender and golden. Stir in the tomato paste and cook 2 minutes.

2. Add the tomatoes and bring to a simmer. Add salt and pepper to taste and cook 1 hour or until the sauce is thickened, stirring occasionally. Stir in the basil.

3. Prepare the filling: Heat the oil in a large skillet over medium heat. Add the meats, garlic, and salt and pepper to taste. Cook 10 minutes, stirring to break up the lumps. When the meat is browned, add two cups of the prepared tomato sauce. Bring to a simmer and cook until thickened, about 20 minutes. Stir in the peas. Let cool slightly.

4. Smear the butter over the bottom and sides of a 13 × 9 × 2-inch baking pan. Coat the pan with the bread crumbs, patting them so that they adhere.

5. Place a rack in the center of the oven. Preheat the oven to 375°F. Bring at least 4 quarts of water to a boil in each of two large

pots. Add 3 tablespoons of salt to each pot, then the pasta. Stir well. Cook over high heat, stirring frequently, until the pasta is tender but slightly underdone. Drain the pasta and return it to the pot. Toss the pasta with 3 cups of the plain tomato sauce and the grated cheeses.

6. Carefully spoon half the pasta into the prepared pan, trying not to disturb the bread crumbs. Spoon the meat filling evenly over the pasta. Scatter the cheese cubes on top. Spoon the remaining pasta over all. Flatten the contents of the pan with a spoon.

7. Have ready a cooling rack and a large tray or cutting board the size of the pan. Bake 60 to 90 minutes or until the pasta is heated through and crusty on top. Let the pasta cool in the pan on the rack 30 minutes. Slide a small knife around the edges of the pan. Protecting your hands with oven mitts, invert the pasta onto the tray or cutting board. Cut into squares and serve warm with the remaining tomato sauce.

Sophia Loren's Baked Pasta

Pasta al Forno alla Loren

Makes 8 to 10 servings

The actress Sophia Loren loves to cook and has even written cookbooks. Her real last name is Scicolone, the same as mine, though my name comes from my husband and his Sicilian family. Sophia is from Naples, like my grandparents, though my maiden name was Scotto. I am often asked if we are related. We are not, though I do admire Sophia's beauty and talent, both as an actress and a cook.

This is my interpretation of a baked pasta recipe I once heard her describe as a favorite dish for company. If you have prepared the dish ahead and stored it in the refrigerator, be sure to add at least a half hour to the baking time.

4 cups Bologna-Style Sauce or other meat and tomato sauce

    4 cups <u>Béchamel Sauce</u>

Salt

1½ pounds penne, ziti, or mostaccioli

1 cup freshly grated Parmigiano-Reggiano

1. Prepare the two sauces, if necessary. Then, butter a 13 × 9 × 2–inch baking pan.

2. Bring at least 4 quarts of water to a boil in a large pot. Add 2 tablespoons of salt, then the pasta. Stir well. Cook over high heat, stirring frequently, until the pasta is almost tender. Drain the pasta.

3. Place a rack in the center of the oven. Preheat the oven to 400°F. Set aside $1/4$ cup of the cheese. Toss the pasta with half of the Bolognese sauce. Spread about $1/3$ of the pasta in the pan. Spoon on about $1/3$ of the Béchamel sauce and cheese. Dot with additional Bolognese sauce.

4. Repeat, adding two more layers, using all of the ingredients. Sprinkle with the reserved cheese.

5. Cover the pan with foil. Bake until bubbling around the edges and the blade of a thin knife inserted into the center feels hot, about 45 minutes. Uncover and bake 15 minutes more. Remove the pasta from the oven. Cool 15 minutes on a wire rack. Serve hot.

Linguine with Clam Sauce

Linguine alle Vongole

Makes 4 to 6 servings

Use the smallest clams you can find, such as Manila clams or littlenecks. New Zealand cockles have become widely available in my area and may have in your area, too. These work well also. Italians use dime-size vongole, *tender, hard-shell clams with beautiful zigzag markings. Either these clams are not very sandy, or they are well cleaned before they are cooked, because Italians do not bother to remove the clams from their shells before making the sauce.*

Linguine with clam sauce should not be served with grated cheese.

3 pounds small hard-shell clams or New Zealand cockles, well scrubbed

⅓ cup extra-virgin olive oil, plus more for drizzling

4 garlic cloves, finely chopped

2 tablespoon chopped fresh flat-leaf parsley

Pinch of crushed red pepper

1 pound linguine

Salt

1. Place the clams in a large pot with $1/4$ cup water over medium-high heat. Cover the pot and cook until the liquid is boiling and the clams begin to open. Remove the opened clams with a slotted spoon and transfer to a bowl. Continue cooking the unopened clams. Discard any that refuse to open. Reserve the clam juices.

2. Working over a small bowl to catch the juices, scrape the clams from the shells, placing them in another bowl. Pour all of the liquid from the pot into the bowl with the juices. If the clams are sandy, rinse them one at a time in the clam juices. Pass the liquid through a fine-mesh strainer lined with cheesecloth.

3. Pour the oil into a skillet large enough to hold the cooked pasta. Add the garlic, parsley, and crushed red pepper. Cook over medium heat until the garlic is golden, about 2 minutes. Add the clam juices. Cook until the liquid is reduced by half. Stir in the clams. Cook 1 minute more.

4. Meanwhile, bring at least 4 quarts of water to a boil in a large pot. Add 2 tablespoons of salt, then the linguine, gently pushing it down until the pasta is completely covered with water. Stir

well. Cook, stirring frequently, until the linguine is al dente, tender yet still firm to the bite. Drain the pasta.

5. Transfer the pasta to the skillet with the sauce and toss well over high heat. Add a drizzle of extra-virgin olive oil and toss again. Serve immediately.

Tuscan Spaghetti with Clams

Spaghetti alla Viareggina

Makes 4 to 6 servings

Here is another version of spaghetti with clams as it is made in Viareggio, on the coast of Tuscany. Onion, wine, and tomatoes give the sauce a more complex flavor.

3 pounds small hard-shell clams or New Zealand cockles, well scrubbed

Salt

⅓ cup olive oil

1 small onion, finely chopped

2 garlic cloves, finely chopped

Pinch of crushed red pepper

1½ cups peeled, seeded, and chopped fresh tomatoes or drained and chopped canned imported Italian tomatoes

½ cup dry white wine

2 tablespoons chopped fresh flat-leaf parsley

1 pound spaghetti or linguine

1. Place the clams in a large pot with $1/4$ cup water over medium-high heat. Cover the pot and cook until the liquid is boiling and the clams begin to open. Remove the opened clams with a slotted spoon and transfer to a bowl. Continue cooking the unopened clams. Discard any that do not open.

2. Working over a small bowl to catch the juices, scrape the clams from the shells, placing them in another bowl. Pour all of the liquid from the pot into the bowl with the juices. If the clams are sandy, rinse them one at a time in the clam juices. Pass the liquid through a fine-mesh strainer lined with cheesecloth.

3. Pour the oil into a large saucepan. Add the onion and cook, stirring frequently, over medium heat until the onion is golden, about 10 minutes. Add the garlic and crushed red pepper and cook 2 minutes more.

4. Stir in the tomatoes, wine, and strained clam juice. Simmer 20 minutes or until the sauce is reduced and thickened.

5. Bring at least 4 quarts of water to a boil in a large pot. Add 2 tablespoons of salt, then the pasta, gently pushing it down until the pasta is completely covered with water. Stir well. Cook over high heat, stirring frequently, until the pasta is al dente, tender

yet still firm to the bite. Set aside some of the cooking water. Drain the pasta.

6. Stir the clams and parsley into the sauce. Add some of the water if needed. In a heated serving bowl, toss the sauce and pasta together. Serve immediately.

Linguine with Anchovies and Spicy Tomato Sauce

Linguine alla Puttanesca

Makes 4 to 6 servings

The usual explanation for the Italian name for this tasty sauce is that it was invented by either Roman or Neapolitan streetwalkers who had little time for cooking but wanted a hot, tasty meal.

¼ cup olive oil

3 garlic cloves, very finely chopped

Pinch of crushed red pepper

1 (28-ounce) can imported Italian peeled tomatoes, drained and chopped

Salt

6 anchovy fillets, chopped

½ cup chopped Gaeta or other mild black olives

2 tablespoons chopped rinsed capers

2 tablespoons chopped fresh flat-leaf parsley

1 pound linguine or spaghetti

1. Pour the oil into a skillet large enough to hold all of the cooked pasta. Add the garlic and the crushed red pepper. Cook until the garlic is golden, about 2 minutes.

2. Add the tomatoes and a pinch of salt. Bring to a simmer and cook 15 to 20 minutes or until the sauce is thickened.

3. Add the anchovies, olives, and capers and simmer 2 to 3 minutes more. Stir in the parsley.

4. Bring at least 4 quarts of water to a boil in a large pot. Add the linguine and salt to taste. Gently push the pasta down until it is completely covered with water. Cook, stirring frequently, until the pasta is al dente, tender yet still firm to the bite. Set aside some of the cooking water. Drain the pasta.

5. Add the pasta to the skillet with the sauce. Toss 1 minute over high heat, adding a little of the cooking water if needed. Serve immediately.

Linguine with Crab and Little Tomatoes

Linguine al Granchio

Makes 4 to 6 servings

In Naples, tiny dried chiles add flavor to many seafood sauces, but use any hot red pepper sparingly, as it can overwhelm the delicacy of the crab meat. The same goes for the garlic, which in this recipe is used just to flavor the cooking oil, then removed before the tomatoes and crab are added.

⅓ cup olive oil

3 large garlic cloves, crushed

Pinch of crushed red pepper

2 pints cherry or grape tomatoes, halved or quartered if large

Salt and freshly ground black pepper

8 ounces fresh lump crabmeat, picked over to remove bits of shell, or chopped cooked lobster

8 fresh basil leaves, torn into bits

1 pound linguine

1. Pour the oil into a large skillet. Add the garlic cloves and red pepper and cook over medium heat, pressing down on the garlic once or twice with the back of a spoon, until the garlic is deep golden, about 4 minutes. Remove the garlic with a slotted spoon.

2. Add the tomatoes and salt and pepper to taste. Cook, stirring frequently, until the tomatoes are softened and have released their juices, about 10 minutes.

3. Gently stir in the crab and basil. Remove from the heat.

4. Bring at least 4 quarts of water to a boil in a large pot. Add 2 tablespoons of salt, then the pasta, gently pushing it down until the pasta is completely covered with water. Stir well. Cook over high heat, stirring frequently, until the linguine is al dente, tender yet still firm to the bite.

5. Drain the pasta, reserving a little of the cooking water. Add the pasta to the pan with the sauce, adding a little of the water if it seems dry. Toss over high heat 1 minute. Serve immediately.

Linguine with Mixed Seafood Sauce

Linguine ai Frutti di Mare

Makes 4 to 6 servings

Sweet little grape tomatoes are full of flavor like the pomodorini della collina, *little hillside tomatoes, grown around Naples. If grape tomatoes are not available, use cherry tomatoes or chopped fresh plum tomatoes instead.*

This sauce can be prepared in the brief time it takes to cook the pasta. To be sure that nothing gets overcooked, have all of the ingredients and needed equipment ready before starting. To save time and effort, you can use precut calamari (squid) rings.

1 pound cleaned calamari (squid)

6 tablespoons extra-virgin olive oil, plus more for drizzling

Salt

1 pound medium shrimp, shelled and deveined

2 large garlic cloves, very finely chopped

¼ cup chopped fresh flat-leaf parsley

Pinch of crushed red pepper

1 pint grape or cherry tomatoes, halved

1 pound small hard-shell clams or mussels, cleaned and shelled as directed in steps 1 and 2 of Linguine with Clam Sauce, including juice

1 pound linguine or thin spaghetti

1. Cut the calamari bodies into $1/2$-inch rings and the base of the tentacles in half crosswise. Cut the shrimp into $1/2$-inch pieces. Pat the seafood dry.

2. In a skillet large enough to hold all of the ingredients, heat 4 tablespoons of the oil over medium-high heat. Add the calamari and salt to taste. Cook, stirring often, until the calamari are just opaque, about 2 minutes. Scoop the calamari out with a slotted spoon and transfer to a plate. Add the shrimp and salt, to taste, to the pan. Cook, stirring, until the shrimp are just pink, about 1 minute. Transfer the shrimp to the plate with the calamari.

3. Add the remaining 2 tablespoons of the oil, and the garlic, parsley, and red pepper to the pan. Cook, stirring, until the garlic is golden, about 2 minutes. Add the tomatoes and clam juice. Cook 5 minutes or until the tomatoes are tender. Stir in the calamari, shrimp and clams.

4. Bring at least 4 quarts of water to a boil in a large pot. Add 2 tablespoons of salt, then the pasta, gently pushing it down until the pasta is completely covered with water. Stir well. Cook over high heat, stirring frequently, until the pasta is al dente, tender yet still firm to the bite. Drain the pasta, reserving some of the cooking water.

5. Add the pasta to the pan with the seafood. Cook over high heat, tossing the pasta with the sauce, for 30 seconds. Add a little cooking water if needed. Drizzle with extra-virgin olive oil and toss again. Serve hot.

Thin Spaghetti with Bottarga

Spaghettini con Bottarga

Makes 4 to 6 servings

Bottarga is the dried salted roe of mullet, tuna, or other fish. Most of it comes from Sardinia or Sicily. It is sold in a whole piece in the refrigerator case of many seafood markets and gourmet shops and shaved or grated with a vegetable peeler or cheese grater. There is also a dried, powdered type that is sold in jars. It is convenient, but I prefer the refrigerated variety. The flavor of bottarga is somewhere between that of caviar and top-quality anchovies.

1/3 cup extra-virgin olive oil

2 garlic cloves, finely chopped

2 tablespoons chopped fresh flat-leaf parsley

Pinch of crushed red pepper

Salt

1 pound thin spaghetti

3 to 4 tablespoons shaved or grated bottarga

1. Pour the oil into a skillet large enough to hold all of the pasta. Add the garlic, parsley, and pepper. Cook over medium heat until the garlic is golden, about 2 minutes.

2. Bring at least 4 quarts of water to a boil in a large pot. Add 2 tablespoons of salt, then the pasta. Stir well, gently pushing the pasta down until it is completely covered with water. Cook over high heat, stirring frequently, until the pasta is al dente, tender yet still firm to the bite. Drain the pasta, reserving some of the cooking water.

3. Add the pasta to the skillet and toss well 1 minute over high heat Add some of the cooking water if needed. Sprinkle with the bottarga and toss again. Serve immediately.

Venetian Whole-Wheat Spaghetti in Anchovy Sauce

Bigoli in Salsa

Makes 4 to 6 servings

In Venice, thick whole-wheat spaghetti is handmade with a special device called a torchio that works something like a meat grinder. The dough is forced through small holes in the torchio and emerges as long strands. For this recipe, which is a Venetian classic, I use dried whole-wheat spaghetti.

¼ cup olive oil

2 medium red onions, halved and thinly sliced

½ cup dry white wine

1 (3-ounce) jar anchovy fillets

Salt

1 pound whole-wheat spaghetti

Freshly ground black pepper

1. Pour the oil into a skillet large enough to hold all of the pasta. Add the onions and cook over medium heat until the onions are golden, about 10 minutes. Add the wine and cook, stirring frequently, until the onions are soft but not browned, about 15 minutes more.

2. Drain the anchovies, reserving the oil. Add the anchovies to the skillet and stir. Cook 10 minutes more, stirring often, until the anchovies dissolve.

3. Bring at least 4 quarts of water to a boil in a large pot. Add 2 tablespoons of salt, then the pasta. Stir well, gently pushing the pasta down until it is completely covered with water. Cook over high heat, stirring frequently, until the pasta is al dente, tender yet still firm to the bite. Set aside some of the cooking water. Drain the pasta.

4. Add the pasta to the pan with the sauce, and toss together 1 minute over high heat, adding a little of the water if needed. Drizzle with some of the reserved anchovy oil if desired, and top with freshly ground pepper. Serve immediately.

Capri-Style Spaghetti

Spaghetti alla Caprese

Makes 4 to 6 servings

Fish and cheese are rarely combined in Italy, because the sharpness of the cheese may overwhelm the delicacy of the fish. But for every rule, there is an exception. Here is a pasta from the island of Capri that combines two types of fish with mozzarella. The flavors work because the cheese is mild and rich, yet easily dominated by the anchovies and tuna.

⅓ cup olive oil

2 cups peeled, seeded, and chopped fresh tomatoes or drained and chopped canned imported Italian tomatoes

Salt

4 anchovy fillets, chopped

1 (7-ounce) can tuna in olive oil, drained and chopped

12 Gaeta or other mild black olives, pitted and chopped

Freshly ground black pepper

1 pound spaghetti

Salt

4 ounces fresh mozzarella, diced

1. In a skillet large enough to hold the cooked pasta, heat the olive oil over medium heat. Add the tomatoes and salt to taste. Cook, stirring occasionally, 10 to 15 minutes or until the tomato juices have evaporated. Turn off the heat.

2. Stir the chopped ingredients into the tomato sauce. Add pepper to taste.

3. Bring at least 4 quarts of water to a boil in a large pot. Add 2 tablespoons of salt, then the pasta. Stir well, gently pushing the pasta down until it is completely covered with water. Cook over high heat, stirring frequently, until the pasta is al dente, tender yet still firm to the bite. Drain the pasta, reserving some of the cooking water.

4. Add the pasta to the pan with the sauce and toss well 1 minute over medium heat. Add a little water if the pasta seems dry. Add the mozzarella and toss again. Serve immediately.

Linguine with Shrimp, Venetian Style

Linguine al Gamberi alla Veneta

Makes 6 servings

Perhaps because their city was once a major trading port with the East, Venetian cooks have always been open to experimentation. This linguine, for example, is flavored with a slice of fresh ginger, which is not often used in Italian cooking but works wonderfully with shrimp.

1½ pounds large shrimp, shelled and deveined

½ cup olive oil

3 garlic cloves, finely chopped

¼-inch thick piece fresh ginger, peeled

Pinch of crushed red pepper

Salt to taste

1 tablespoon fresh lemon juice

1 cup dry white wine

2 tablespoons chopped fresh flat-leaf parsley

1 pound linguine

1. Rinse the shrimp and pat them dry. Cut each shrimp into $1/2$-inch pieces.

2. Pour the oil into a skillet large enough to hold all of the cooked pasta. Add the garlic, ginger, and crushed red pepper. Cook over medium heat until the garlic is golden, about 2 minutes. Add the shrimp and a big pinch of salt. Cook, stirring, until the shrimp are cooked through, about 2 minutes. Add the lemon juice and wine and bring to a simmer. Cook 2 minutes. Stir in the parsley. Remove from the heat.

3. Bring at least 4 quarts of water to a boil in a large pot. Add 2 tablespoons of salt, then the pasta. Stir well, gently pushing the pasta down until it is completely covered with water. Cook over high heat, stirring frequently, until the pasta is al dente, tender yet still firm to the bite. Drain the pasta, reserving some of the cooking water.

4. Add the pasta to the skillet and toss over high heat 1 minute until well mixed. Add a little of the cooking water if needed. Remove the ginger. Serve immediately.

Pasta with Sardines and Fennel

Pasta con le Sarde

Makes 6 servings

Sicilians are passionate about this dish, and every cook claims to have the best and most authentic recipe. Some add tomatoes, and some stew the sardines along with the fennel, but I prefer this method of cooking the sardines separately and layering them with the pasta and saving the tomatoes for another recipe.

Fennel grows wild all over Sicily, and the green fronds are used to make this pasta. Cultivated fennel does not have the same flavor, but the wild fennel is not widely available here. I use a combination of fresh dill and cultivated fennel to approximate the flavor of this classic Sicilian dish. Toasted bread crumbs, not cheese, are the appropriate topping.

2 medium fennel bulbs, trimmed and sliced

1 cup chopped fresh dill

1/2 teaspoon saffron threads

1/2 cup plus 1 tablespoon olive oil

¼ cup plain dry bread crumbs

1 pound fresh sardines, cleaned and filleted (see Note)

Salt and freshly ground black pepper

1 large onion, chopped

6 anchovy fillets

½ cup dried currants

½ cup pine nuts

1 pound perciatelli or bucatini

1. Bring at least 4 quarts of water to a boil in a large pot. Add the fennel and dill and cook until tender when pierced with a fork, about 10 minutes. Scoop out the fennel and dill with a slotted spoon, reserving the cooking water. Let the fennel and dill cool, then finely chop them. In a small bowl, soak the saffron threads in 2 tablespoons of the fennel water.

2. In a small skillet, heat 1 tablespoon of the oil over medium heat and cook the bread crumbs, stirring constantly, until toasted, about 5 minutes.

3. In a large skillet, heat $1/4$ cup of the oil. Fry the sardines cut-side down first in the oil until cooked through, about 1 minute on each side. Sprinkle with salt and pepper. Transfer the sardines to a plate.

4. Wipe out the skillet. Pour the remaining $1/4$ cup of the oil into the skillet. Add the onion and cook over medium heat until golden, about 10 minutes. Add the anchovies, currants, pine nuts, saffron, and salt and pepper to taste. Cook, stirring often, 10 minutes.

5. Add the fennel and dill to the onion with one cup of the cooking water. Cook, stirring, 10 minutes.

6. Add more water to the pot to equal 4 quarts of water for cooking the pasta. Bring the water to a boil. Add 2 tablespoons of salt, then the pasta. Stir well, gently pushing the pasta down until it is completely covered with water. Cook over high heat, stirring frequently, until the pasta is al dente, tender yet still firm to the bite. Drain the pasta.

7. Transfer the pasta to the skillet with the fennel mixture and toss well. Spoon half the pasta into a warm serving bowl. Layer with half of the sardines. Add the remaining pasta. Sprinkle with the bread crumbs and top with the sardines. Serve immediately.

Penne with Zucchini, Swordfish, and Herbs

Penne con Zucchine e Pesce Spada

Makes 4 to 6 servings

This pasta is inspired by one I saw in a favorite Italian cooking magazine, A Tavola ("at the table"), in a story about cooking at a beach house. The zest and herbs make the dish light and fresh. It is perfect on a summer day—even if you're not at the beach—followed by a tomato salad.

¼ cup olive oil

12 ounces swordfish, trimmed and cut into ½-inch cubes

Salt and freshly ground black pepper

4 to 6 small zucchini, about 1 pound, cut into ½-inch pieces

4 green onions, chopped

2 tablespoons chopped fresh rosemary

2 tablespoons chopped fresh chives

1 tablespoon chopped fresh mint

½ teaspoon dried oregano, crumbled

½ teaspoon grated lemon zest

1 pound penne

1. In a large skillet, heat 1 tablespoon oil over medium heat. Add the swordfish and cook until the fish loses its pink color, about 5 minutes. Remove the swordfish and transfer to a plate. Sprinkle with salt and pepper.

2. Add the remaining 3 tablespoons oil to the pan and heat over medium heat. Add the zucchini, green onions, and salt to taste. Cook, stirring often, until the zucchini are just tender, about 10 minutes.

3. Return the swordfish to the pan. Stir in the herbs and lemon zest and remove from the heat.

4. Bring at least 4 quarts of water to a boil in a large pot. Add 2 tablespoons of salt, then the pasta. Stir well. Cook over high heat, stirring frequently, until the pasta is al dente, tender yet still firm to the bite. Drain the pasta, reserving some of the cooking water.

5. Add the pasta to the skillet and toss over high heat 1 minute to combine. Add some of the reserved pasta water, if needed. Serve immediately.

Christmas Eve Spaghetti with Baccala

Spaghetti con la Baccala

Makes 6 servings

Baccala is an important part of the all-fish menu served in most southern Italian homes on Christmas Eve. This recipe was given to me by my aunt, Millie Castagliola, whose family came from Sicily. Aunt Millie makes this same sauce as a filling for a double-crust pizza.

1 pound stockfish or baccala,

Salt

¼ cup olive oil

2 medium onions, thinly sliced

2 celery ribs, thinly sliced

2 garlic cloves, finely chopped

2 cups chopped canned imported Italian tomatoes with their juice

Pinch of crushed red pepper

½ cup sliced green olives

2 tablespoons capers, rinsed and drained

1 pound spaghetti or linguine

Extra-virgin olive oil

1. Bring about 1 quart of water to a boil in a wide saucepan. Add the fish and salt to taste. Reduce the heat to low. Simmer the fish until very tender, about 10 minutes. Remove the fish with a slotted spoon. Let cool slightly. With your fingers, remove any skin and bones. Cut the fish into bite-size pieces.

2. Pour the oil into a large saucepan. Add the onions and celery and cook over medium heat until the vegetables are golden, about 15 minutes. Stir in the garlic and cook 2 minutes more.

3. Add the tomatoes and red pepper. Cook, stirring occasionally, until the sauce is thick, 20 to 30 minutes.

4. Add the fish, olives, and capers and cook 10 minutes. Taste for salt.

5. Bring at least 4 quarts of water to a boil in a large pot. Add 2 tablespoons of salt, then the pasta. Stir well, gently pushing the pasta down until it is completely covered with water. Cook, stirring frequently, until the pasta is al dente, tender yet still firm to the bite. Drain the pasta, reserving a little of the cooking water.

6. Add the pasta to the pan with the sauce. Toss well over medium heat, adding a little of the cooking water if needed. Drizzle with a little extra- virgin olive oil and serve immediately.

Linguine with Tuna Pesto

Linguine al Tonno

Makes 4 to 6 servings

The uncooked sauce for this Sicilian pasta is similar to pesto, but flavored with anchovies. Just before serving, the sauce and pasta are tossed with canned tuna.

1 cup tightly packed fresh basil leaves

¾ cup tightly packed fresh parsley leaves

⅓ cup pine nuts

2 medium garlic cloves

1 (2-ounce) can anchovy fillets, drained

⅓ cup extra-virgin olive oil

2 tablespoons fresh lemon juice

1 (7-ounce) can tuna in oil (preferably imported Italian or Spanish tuna in olive oil)

Salt

1 pound linguine

1. In a food processor fitted with the steel blade, chop the basil, parsley, pine nuts, and garlic until fine. Add the anchovy fillets, oil, and lemon juice and process until smooth.

2. Bring at least 4 quarts of water to a boil in a large pot. Meanwhile, in a large serving bowl, mash the tuna with a fork. Stir in the sauce.

3. Add 2 tablespoons of salt, then the pasta, to the boiling water. Stir well, gently pushing the pasta down until it is completely covered with water. Cook the pasta, stirring frequently, until al dente, tender yet still firm to the bite. Drain the pasta, reserving some of the cooking water.

4. Transfer the pasta to the bowl with the sauce. Add some of the cooking water and toss well. Serve immediately.

Cold Pasta with Vegetable Confetti and Seafood

Pasta Fredda con Verdure e Crostacei

Makes 6 to 8 servings

On one trip to Italy, the main reason I visited Argenta, a small town in Emilia-Romagna, was to dine at a fine restaurant called Il Trigabolo. The restaurant is closed now, but I still remember my delight when they served me this refreshing cold pasta, crunchy with bits of chopped vegetables and seafood. Most of the vegetables are blanched—that is, they are dropped into the boiling water, then immediately placed under cold water to stop the cooking and cool them. The cool water sets their bright color, and the vegetables keep some of their crunchy texture.

Pasta should be rinsed in cool water only in a preparation like this—when you want to stop the cooking and serve the pasta cold.

1 large firm ripe tomato, cored and diced

½ pound cooked small shrimp, cut into ¼-inch pieces

1 cup chopped cooked lobster or ¼ pound cooked crabmeat, picked over

¼ cup snipped fresh chives

¼ cup chopped fresh basil

¼ cup extra-virgin olive oil, plus more for drizzling

Coarse salt and freshly ground black pepper

1 pound thin spaghetti

¾ cup very finely chopped red bell pepper

¾ cup very finely chopped yellow bell pepper

¾ cup very finely chopped zucchini

2 small carrots, cut into matchstick strips

1. In a large serving bowl, combine the tomato with the shrimp, lobster, herbs, and olive oil. Season with salt and pepper.

2. Bring at least 4 quarts of water to a boil in a large pot. Add 2 tablespoons of salt, then the spaghetti. Stir well, gently pushing the pasta down until it is completely covered with water. Cook over high heat, stirring frequently. About 30 seconds before the pasta is ready, add the peppers, zucchini, and carrots. Stir well. As soon as the pasta is al dente, tender yet still firm to the bite, drain it and the vegetables into a large colander placed in the sink. The vegetables will be just slightly wilted.

3. Rinse the pasta and vegetables under cool running water. Drain well.

4. Add the pasta to the tomato and seafood mixture. Toss well. Drizzle with additional oil and toss again. Serve immediately.

Fresh Egg Pasta

Pasta al Uovo

Makes about 1 pound

Here is a basic all-purpose pasta dough that I use for fettuccine, lasagne, and ravioli. The dough can be assembled by hand, in a food processor, or in a heavy-duty mixer, and it can be rolled out on a board with a rolling pin or in a pasta rolling machine. If you have never made pasta before, read the recipe through before beginning. The most important thing is to get the balance of flour and eggs right so that the dough is neither sticky nor dry. Because the freshness and size of the eggs and the type and humidity level of the flour vary slightly, it is not possible to give exact proportions.

Making fresh pasta is as easy as making any other dough, but it does take some patience. Make it ahead of time, if you like. It keeps well at cool room temperature up to a week, or it can be refrigerated or frozen. A small amount of olive oil helps to keep the dough moist as you work.

About 2½ cups unbleached all-purpose flour

4 large eggs, beaten

1 teaspoon olive oil (optional, but a good idea, especially for stuffed pastas)

Preparing the Dough by Hand

1. Pour the flour into a mound on a countertop or large pasta board. A rough surface such as wood or plastic is better than a smooth one such as marble or granite. With a fork, make a wide hole in the center of the mound. Pour the eggs and olive oil into the hole and begin stirring with one hand, gradually incorporating some of the flour from the inside of the hole. Use your other hand to support the wall of flour surrounding the eggs, so they don't spill out.

2. When the dough forms a ball and becomes too firm to stir, in about 1 minute, sweep the remaining flour to one side. Lightly flour your hands and begin kneading. Push the dough away with the heels of your hands and pull it back toward you with your fingertips. Turn the dough as you are doing this for even kneading. Continue kneading, gradually incorporating some of the remaining flour until the ball becomes somewhat smooth, feels moist, and is only slightly sticky, about 3 minutes. Add only enough flour to create a firm ball of dough, or it may become too dry.

3. Put the dough aside for a moment and cover it with an inverted bowl. Wash and dry your hands to remove hardened scraps of dough. Scrape the kneading surface clean with a plastic or metal dough scraper or spatula to remove any hardened pieces of dough and excess flour that might later cause lumps. Throw out the scraps.

4. Lightly dust your hands with flour. Resume kneading the dough until it is smooth and elastic, moist yet not sticky, about 8 to 10 minutes. Add more flour if necessary. There should be no streaks of flour on the dough, and the color should be evenly yellow. The more the dough is kneaded, the lighter and more resilient the pasta will be, so do not skimp on kneading. Work quickly so that the dough does not dry out.

Making the Dough with a Food Processor or Heavy-Duty Mixer

1. Pour the eggs and olive oil into a food processor fitted with the steel blade, or into the bowl of a heavy-duty electric mixer fitted with the flat beater. With the machine running, begin adding the flour a tablespoon at a time. Mix until the dough forms a ball and cleans the inside of the bowl, about 1 minute. Pinch the dough. It should feel moist but not sticky and should be fairly smooth. If not, add more flour as needed.

2. Place the dough on a lightly floured surface and knead it for 1 minute, adding more flour if necessary, until it is firm, smooth without streaks of flour, and moist but not sticky.

> **Spinach Pasta:** Pasta made with fresh spinach has not only a bright green color but also a good flavor. To make fresh spinach pasta, use 3 cups flour, 3 large eggs, and 1 pound of fresh spinach, cooked, squeezed dry, and very finely chopped (about $3/4$ cup cooked spinach). Combine the ingredients as for Fresh Egg Pasta at left. Makes about $1^{1}/_{4}$ pounds of pasta.

Letting the Dough Rest

Whether you have made it by hand or machine, cover the dough with an inverted bowl and let it rest for 30 minutes or up to 2 hours at room temperature.

Rolling Out the Dough By Hand

1. Lightly dust a countertop or large board with flour. Be sure that the surface is perfectly flat and not warped.

2. Cut the dough into 2 pieces. It may feel moister after it rests because the eggs have absorbed the flour. While you work with one piece, keep the remainder covered. With your hands, shape one piece of dough into a disk. Choose a wooden rolling pin at least 24 inches long and $1^{1}/_{2}$ to 2 inches wide and dust it lightly with flour. Place the pin in the center and push it away from you

toward the edge of the dough. Rotate the dough a quarter turn, center the pin on it and push it toward the edge once more. Repeat, rotating the dough and rolling it out from the center, keeping the shape round and the thickness even, until the dough reaches the desired thinness. Flip the dough over from time to time to be sure it is not sticking. If necessary, dust lightly with flour.

3. Work quickly so that the dough does not dry out. If it should tear, pinch it together or patch it with a small piece of dough from the edge. The dough is ready when it is very thin and you can easily see your hand through it when it is held up to the light. Roll out the remaining dough in the same way. Be sure to make all of the dough pieces of equal thickness. Turn the pieces often so that they do not stick. If the dough will be used to make stuffed pasta such as ravioli, it should be kept covered so that it remains pliable. Use it as soon as possible.

4. Cut the dough into the desired size and shape while it is still soft and pliable. See the various pasta recipes in sections <u>Fresh Pasta</u>, <u>Lasagne</u>, and <u>Stuffed Fresh Pasta</u> for instructions on cutting and shaping the dough.

Rolling Out the Dough with a Pasta Machine

1. Following the manufacturer's instructions, clamp the pasta machine to one end of a large countertop or sturdy table. Set the rollers at the widest opening and dust them lightly with flour.

2. Cut the dough into 4 to 6 pieces. It may feel moister after it rests because the eggs have absorbed the flour. While you work with one piece, keep the remainder covered. Flatten one piece of dough into an oval disk. Turn the handle of the pasta machine with one hand while the other guides the piece of dough through the rollers. If the dough sticks or tears, dust it lightly with flour.

3. Remove the dough from the machine and fold it lengthwise into thirds. Pass the dough through the machine again, flouring it if necessary.

4. Close the rollers slightly by moving the dial to the next notch. Pass the dough through the rollers. As the dough emerges, lift it straight out so that it stays flat without wrinkling. Do not fold it.

5. Continue to pass the dough through the machine, moving the dial up one notch each time until the desired thinness is reached. This will vary according to the machine, but I usually stop at the second-to-last setting for fettuccine and flat pasta and the last notch for stuffed pasta. The pasta should be thin enough that you can see your hand through it without tearing. Don't be

tempted to re-roll scraps of dough. Hardened edges can stick in the machine and tear the pasta.

6. Lay the strip of dough on a lightly floured kitchen towel. Roll out the remaining dough in the same way. Be sure to make all of the strips of equal thickness. Turn the pieces often so that they do not stick. If the dough will be used to make stuffed pasta such as ravioli, it should be kept covered so that it remains pliable. Use it as soon as possible.

7. Cut the dough into the desired size and shape while it is still soft and pliable. See the various pasta recipes in sections <u>Fresh Pasta</u>, <u>Lasagne</u>, and <u>Stuffed Fresh Pasta</u> for instructions on cutting and shaping the dough.

Making Pasta Noodles

Lasagne, papardelle, fettuccine, tagliatelle, and tagliarini are all flat ribbons of pasta. Their use depends on the type of sauce you are making and regional preferences. Generally, the lighter the sauce, the narrower the pasta.

1. Make the pasta as described for <u>Fresh Egg Pasta</u>.

2. Let the dough dry until it is slightly leathery but still pliable, about 20 minutes.

3. If using your pasta machine's cutting attachment, follow the manufacturer's instructions. Turn the crank with one hand, passing the sheet of dough through the cutters. As the dough emerges, lift it straight out with your other hand so that the strands do not collect on the countertop and become wrinkled.

4. If working by hand, first cut the dough into 5-inch lengths for pappardelle and 10-inch lengths for the other pastas. Loosely roll up a strip of dough. With a large heavy chef's knife, cut the rolled up pasta crosswise into strips 3 inches wide for lasagne, $3/4$ inches wide for papardelle, $1/3$ inch wide for fettuccine, $1/4$ inch for tagliatelle, and $1/8$ inch for tagliarini. Separate the strips and place them flat on a floured surface to dry about 1 hour at room temperature.

Storing Fresh Egg Pasta

Fresh pasta may be used immediately, frozen, or allowed to dry completely. To freeze the pasta, place the strips on baking sheets lightly dusted with flour so that they do not touch. Place the baking sheets in the freezer. When the pasta is firm, gently gather it into a bundle and wrap it well in layers of plastic wrap or foil. Store in the freezer up to one month.

To dry, place the pasta strips, not touching, on baking sheets. Cover each sheet with lightweight cloth kitchen towels. Do not cover them with plastic or foil or they will turn moldy. Leave the strips at room temperature for several days until the pieces are completely dry and snap when broken. Store in plastic bags in the pantry until ready to use.

Fettuccine with Butter and Parmigiano

Fettuccine al Burro

Makes 4 to 6 servings

Even the pickiest children love fresh egg pasta tossed with butter and cheese. Keep in mind that fresh pasta cooks quickly; it will get mushy fast if you walk away.

6 tablespoons unsalted butter

1 pound fresh fettuccine

Salt

1 cup freshly grated Parmigiano-Reggiano

Freshly ground black pepper

1. Melt the butter in a small saucepan and keep warm.

2. Bring at least 4 quarts of water to a boil. Add the pasta and salt to taste. Stir well. Cook over high heat, stirring frequently, until the pasta is al dente, tender yet firm to the bite. Drain the pasta, reserving some of the cooking water.

3. Pour the pasta into a warm serving bowl. Add half the cheese and toss well. Add the butter and a little of the cooking water if the pasta seems dry. Sprinkle with the remaining cheese and toss again. Sprinkle with freshly ground pepper if desired.

Fettuccine with Butter and Cheese

Fettuccine all'Alfredo

Makes 6 to 8 servings

In the early 1910s Alfredo Di Lelio, whose family owned a trattoria in Rome, created this rich pasta dish of fresh fettuccine, butter, and Parmigiano. The dish became so popular that Alfredo was soon running a bigger, fancier restaurant under his own name, where he would prepare the pasta at tableside, serving it up to diners with great fanfare and a gold fork and spoon. Silent movie stars Douglas Fairbanks, Sr., and his wife, Mary Pickford, were said to have been among the restaurant's many famous patrons.

This recipe was given to me by Russell Bellanca, owner of the Alfredo The Original of Rome Restaurants in New York City and Epcot Center, Florida. According to Russell, this is the recipe as developed by Alfredo Di Lelio. His son, Alfredo II, gave it to Russell's dad, who was a business partner many years ago. At Alfredo The Original, the pasta is handmade from a mix of three different flours and organic egg yolks, though I use my own homemade pasta.

Serve the pasta in small portions. It is very rich.

1½ sticks (¾ cup) unsalted butter, at room temperature for at least 30 minutes

1 cup freshly grated Parmigiano-Reggiano, plus more for serving (optional)

1 pound fresh fettuccine

Salt

1. In a large bowl with an electric mixer, beat the butter with the cheese until it forms a smooth cream, about 2 minutes.

2. Bring at least 4 quarts of water to a boil. Add the pasta and salt to taste. Stir well. Cook over high heat, stirring frequently, until the pasta is al dente, tender yet still firm to the bite. Drain the pasta, reserving a little of the cooking water. Toss the pasta with the butter and cheese and a few tablespoons of the cooking water.

3. Serve immediately with additional cheese, if desired.

EXTRA DESSERT RECIPES

Summer Fruit Torte

Torta dell'Estate

Makes 8 servings

Soft stone fruits such as plums, apricots, peaches, and nectarines are ideal for this torte. Try making it with a combination of fruits.

12 to 16 prune plums or apricots, or 6 medium peaches or nectarines, halved, pitted, and cut into ½-inch slices

1 cup all-purpose flour

1 teaspoon baking powder

½ teaspoon salt

½ cup (1 stick) unsalted butter, at room temperature

⅔ cup plus 2 tablespoons sugar

1 large egg

1 teaspoon grated lemon zest

1 teaspoon pure vanilla extract

Confectioner's sugar

1. Place the rack in the center of the oven. Preheat the oven to 350°F. Grease a 9-inch springform pan.

2. In a large bowl, mix together the flour, baking powder, and salt.

3. In another large bowl, beat the butter with $2/3$ cup of the sugar until light and fluffy, about 3 minutes. Beat in the egg, lemon zest, and vanilla until smooth. Add the dry ingredients and stir just until blended, about 1 minute more.

4. Scrape the batter into the prepared pan. Arrange the fruit, overlapping it slightly, on top in concentric circles. Sprinkle with the remaining 2 tablespoons of sugar.

5. Bake 45 to 50 minutes or until the cake is golden brown and a toothpick inserted in the center comes out clean.

6. Let the cake cool in the pan on a wire rack 10 minutes, then remove the rim of the pan. Let the cake cool completely. Sprinkle with confectioner's sugar before serving. Serve immediately, or cover with an overturned bowl and store at room temperature up to 24 hours.

Autumn Fruit Torte

Torta del Autunno

Makes 8 servings

Apples, pears, figs, or plums are good in this simple cake. The batter forms a top layer that does not quite cover the fruit, allowing it to peek through the surface of the cake. I like to serve it slightly warm.

1½ cups all-purpose flour

1 teaspoon baking powder

½ teaspoon salt

2 large eggs

1 cup sugar

1 teaspoon pure vanilla extract

4 tablespoons unsalted butter, melted and cooled

2 medium apples or pears, peeled, cored, and sliced into thin wedges

Confectioner's sugar

1. Place the rack in the center of the oven. Preheat the oven to 350°F. Grease and flour a 9-inch springform cake pan. Tap out the excess flour.

2. In a bowl, stir together the flour, baking powder, and salt.

3. In a large bowl, beat the eggs with the sugar and vanilla until blended, about 2 minutes. Beat in the butter. Stir in the flour mixture until just blended, about 1 minute more.

4. Spread half of the batter in the prepared pan. Cover with the fruits. Drop the remaining batter on top by spoonfuls. Spread the batter evenly over the fruits. The layer will be thin. Don't be concerned if the fruit is not completely covered.

5. Bake 30 to 35 minutes or until the cake is golden brown and a toothpick inserted in the center comes out clean.

6. Let the cake cool 10 minutes in the pan on a wire rack. Remove the rim of the pan. Cool the cake completely on the rack. Serve warm or at room temperature with a sprinkle of confectioner's sugar. Store covered with a large inverted bowl at room temperature up to 24 hours.

Polenta and Pear Cake

Dolce di Polenta

Makes 8 servings

Yellow cornmeal adds a pleasant texture and warm golden color to this rustic cake from the Veneto.

1 cup all-purpose flour

⅓ cup finely ground yellow cornmeal

1 teaspoon baking powder

½ teaspoon salt

¾ cup (1½ sticks) unsalted butter, softened

¾ cup plus 2 tablespoons sugar

1 teaspoon pure vanilla extract

½ teaspoon grated lemon zest

2 large eggs

⅓ cup milk

1 large ripe pear, cored and thinly sliced

1. Place a rack in the center of the oven. Preheat the oven to 350°F. Grease and flour a 9-inch springform pan. Tap out the excess flour.

2. In a large bowl, sift together the flour, cornmeal, baking powder, and salt.

3. In a large bowl with an electric mixer, beat the butter, gradually adding $3/4$ cup of the sugar until light and fluffy, about 3 minutes. Beat in the vanilla and lemon zest. Beat in the eggs one at time, scraping the sides of the bowl. On low speed, stir in half of the dry ingredients. Add the milk. Stir in the remaining dry ingredients just until smooth, about 1 minute.

4. Spread the batter in the prepared pan. Arrange the pear slices on top, overlapping them slightly. Sprinkle the pear with the remaining 2 tablespoons of sugar.

5. Bake 45 minutes or until the cake is golden brown and a toothpick inserted in the center comes out clean.

6. Cool the cake in the pan 10 minutes on a wire rack. Remove the pan rim and cool the cake completely on the rack. Serve immediately, or cover with a large inverted bowl and store at room temperature up to 24 hours.

Ricotta Cheesecake

Torta di Ricotta

Makes 12 servings

I like to think of this as an American-style Italian cheesecake. It is a large cake, though the flavor is delicate, with lemon zest and cinnamon. This cake is baked in a water bath so that it cooks evenly. The base of the pan is wrapped in foil to prevent the water from seeping into the pan.

1¼ cups sugar

⅓ cup all-purpose flour

½ teaspoon ground cinnamon

3 pounds whole or part-skim ricotta

8 large eggs

2 teaspoons pure vanilla extract

2 teaspoons grated lemon zest

1. Place a rack in the center of the oven. Preheat the oven to 350°F. Grease and flour a 9-inch springform pan. Tap out the excess flour. Place the pan on a 12-inch square of heavy-duty aluminum foil. Mold the foil tightly around the base and about 2 inches up the sides of the pan so that water cannot seep in.

2. In a medium bowl, stir together the sugar, flour, and cinnamon.

3. In a large mixing bowl, whisk the ricotta until smooth. Beat in the eggs, vanilla, and lemon zest until well blended. (For a smoother texture, beat the ingredients with an electric mixer or process them in a food processor.) Whisk in the dry ingredients just until blended.

4. Pour the batter into the prepared pan. Set the pan in a large roasting pan and place it in the oven. Carefully pour hot water to a depth of 1 inch in the roasting pan. Bake $1^1/_2$ hours or until the top of the cake is golden and a toothpick inserted 2 inches from the center comes out clean.

5. Turn off the oven and prop the door open slightly. Let the cake cool in the turned off oven 30 minutes. Remove the cake from the oven and remove the foil wrapping. Cool to room temperature in the pan on a wire rack.

6. Serve at room temperature or refrigerate and serve slightly chilled. Store covered with an inverted bowl in the refrigerator up to 3 days.

Sicilian Ricotta Cake

Cassata

Makes 10 to 12 servings

Cassata is the glory of Sicilian desserts. It consists of two layers of pan di Spagna (Sponge Cake) filled with sweetened, flavored ricotta. The whole cake is frosted with two icings, one of tinted almond paste and the other flavored with lemon. Sicilians decorate the cake with glistening candied fruits and almond paste cutouts so that it looks like something out of a fairy tale.

Originally served only at Easter time, cassata is now found at celebrations throughout the year.

    2 Sponge Cake layers

1 pound whole or part-skim ricotta

½ cup confectioner's sugar

1 teaspoon pure vanilla extract

¼ teaspoon ground cinnamon

½ cup chopped semisweet chocolate

2 tablespoons chopped candied orange peel

Icing

4 ounces almond paste

2 or 3 drops green food coloring

2 egg whites

¼ teaspoon grated lemon zest

1 tablespoon fresh lemon juice

2 cups confectioner's sugar

Candied or dried fruits, such as cherries, pineapple, or citron

1. Prepare the sponge cake, if necessary. Then, in a large bowl with a wire whisk, beat the ricotta, sugar, vanilla, and cinnamon until smooth and creamy. Fold in the chocolate and orange peel.

2. Place one cake layer on a serving plate. Spread the ricotta mixture on top. Place the second cake layer over the filling.

3. For the decoration, crumble the almond paste into a food processor fitted with the steel blade. Add one drop of the food coloring. Process until evenly tinted a light green, adding more

color if needed. Remove the almond paste and shape it into a short thick log.

4. Cut the almond paste into 4 lengthwise slices. Place one slice between two sheets of wax paper. With a rolling pin, flatten it into a narrow ribbon 3 inches long and $1/8$-inch thick. Unwrap and trim off any rough edges, reserving the scraps. Repeat with the remaining almond paste. The ribbons should be about the same width as the height of the cake. Wrap the almond paste ribbons end to end all around the sides of the cake, overlapping the ends slightly.

5. Gather the scraps of almond paste and reroll them. Cut into decorative shapes, such as stars, flowers, or leaves, with cookie cutters.

6. Prepare the icing: Whisk the egg whites, lemon zest, and juice. Add the confectioner's sugar and stir until smooth.

7. Spread the icing evenly over the top of the cake. Decorate the cake with the almond paste cutouts and the candied fruits. Cover with a large overturned bowl and refrigerate until serving time, up to 8 hours. Store leftovers covered in the refrigerator up to 2 days.

Ricotta Crumb Cake

Sbriciolata di Ricotta

Makes 8 servings

Brunch, a very American meal, is fashionable right now in Milan and other cities in northern Italy. This is my version of the ricotta-filled crumb cake I ate at brunch at a caffè not far from the Piazza del Duomo in the heart of Milan.

2½ cups all-purpose flour

½ teaspoon salt

½ teaspoon ground cinnamon

¾ cup (1½ sticks) unsalted butter

⅔ cup sugar

1 large egg

Filling

1 pound whole or part-skim ricotta

¼ cup sugar

1 teaspoon grated lemon zest

1 large egg, beaten

¼ cup raisins

Confectioner's sugar

1. Place a rack in the center of the oven. Preheat the oven to 350°F. Grease and flour a 9-inch springform pan. Tap out the excess flour.

2. In a large bowl, stir together the flour, salt, and cinnamon.

3. In a large bowl, with an electric mixer at medium speed, beat together the butter and sugar until light and fluffy, about 3 minutes. Beat in the egg. On low speed, stir in the dry ingredients until the mixture is blended and forms a firm dough, about 1 minute more.

4. Prepare the filling: Stir together the ricotta, sugar, and lemon zest until blended. Add the egg and stir well. Stir in the raisins.

5. Crumble ⅔ of the dough into the prepared pan. Pat the crumbs firmly to form the bottom crust. Spread with the ricotta mixture, leaving a ½-inch border all around. Crumble the remaining dough over the top, scattering the crumbs evenly.

6. Bake 40 to 45 minutes or until the cake is golden brown and a toothpick inserted in the center comes out clean. Let cool in the pan on a rack 10 minutes.

7. Run a thin metal spatula around the inside of the pan. Remove the pan rim and cool the cake completely. Sprinkle with confectioner's sugar before serving. Store covered with a large inverted bowl in the refrigerator up to 2 days.

Stuffed Rice Timbale

Sartù di Riso

Makes 8 to 10 servings

Rice is not a common ingredient in the Neapolitan kitchen, but this dish is one of the classics of that area. It is believed to have its roots in the aristocratic kitchens run by French-trained chefs when Naples was the capital of the Kingdom of the Two Sicilies.

Today, it is made for special occasions, and I have even eaten contemporary versions made in individual-size molds.

This is the kind of spectacular dish that would be ideal for a party. The little meatballs and other ingredients in the filling come tumbling out of the giant rice cake when it is cut. It is not difficult to make, but there are several steps involved. You can make the sauce and filling up to 3 days ahead of assembling the dish.

Sauce

1 ounce dried porcini mushrooms

2 cups warm water

1 medium onion, chopped

2 tablespoons olive oil

1 (28-ounce) can imported Italian peeled tomatoes, passed through a food mill

Salt and freshly ground black pepper

Meatballs and sausages

2 to 3 slices Italian bread, torn into bits (about ½ cup)

¼ cup milk

8 ounces ground veal

¼ cup freshly grated Parmigiano-Reggiano

1 garlic clove, finely chopped

2 tablespoons chopped fresh flat-leaf parsley, plus more for garnish

1 large egg

Salt and freshly ground black pepper

2 tablespoons olive oil

2 sweet Italian sausages

Assembly

8 ounces fresh mozzarella, chopped

1 cup fresh or frozen peas

2 cups medium-grain rice, such as Arborio, Carnaroli, or Vialone Nano

Salt

1 cup freshly grated Parmigiano-Reggiano

Freshly ground black pepper

2 tablespoons unsalted butter

6 tablespoons plain dry bread crumbs

Chopped fresh flat-leaf parsley for garnish

1. Prepare the sauce: In a medium bowl, soak the mushrooms in the water for 30 minutes. Lift the mushrooms out of the soaking liquid. Strain the liquid through a paper coffee filter or a piece of dampened cheesecloth into a clean bowl and set aside. Rinse the mushrooms under running water, paying special attention to the base where soil collects. Finely chop the mushrooms.

2. Put the onion and oil in a wide heavy saucepan over medium heat. Cook, stirring occasionally until the onion is tender and

golden, about 10 minutes. Stir in the chopped mushrooms. Add the tomatoes and the reserved mushroom liquid. Season to taste with salt and pepper. Bring to a simmer. Cook over low heat, stirring occasionally, until thickened, about 30 minutes.

3. Prepare the meatballs: In a medium bowl, soak the bread in the milk for 5 minutes and squeeze dry. In the same bowl, combine the bread, veal, cheese, garlic, parsley, egg, and salt and pepper to taste. Mix well. Shape the mixture into 1-inch meatballs.

4. In a large skillet, heat the oil over medium heat. Add the meatballs and cook, turning them with tongs, until browned on all sides. With a slotted spoon, transfer the meatballs to a plate. Pour off the oil and carefully wipe out the skillet with paper towels.

5. In the same skillet, combine the sausages and enough water to cover them halfway. Cover and cook over medium-low heat until the water evaporates and the sausages begin to brown. Uncover and cook the sausages, turning them occasionally, until cooked through, about 10 minutes. Cut the sausages into slices.

6. In a medium bowl, gently stir together the meatballs, sausage slices, mozzarella, and peas with 2 cups of the tomato and mushroom sauce and set aside.

7. In a large pot, combine the remaining sauce with 4 cups water. Bring the mixture to a boil. Add the rice and 1 teaspoon of salt. Bring the liquid back to the boil and stir once or twice. Cover and cook over low heat until the rice is barely tender, about 15 minutes.

8. Remove the pot from the heat. Let the rice cool slightly. Stir in the Parmigiano. Season to taste with salt and pepper.

9. Butter the inside of a deep $2^1/_2$-quart casserole dish or ovenproof bowl. Sprinkle it with 4 tablespoons of the bread crumbs. Spoon about two-thirds of the rice into the prepared casserole dish, pressing it against the bottom and sides to make a rice "shell." Spoon the meatball and sausage mixture into the center. Cover with the remaining rice and spread evenly. Sprinkle the top with the remaining crumbs. (If not preparing right away, cover and refrigerate the timbale.)

10. About 2 hours before serving, place a rack in the center of the oven. Preheat the oven to 350°F. Bake the timbale $1^1/_2$ hours or until the surface is lightly browned and the mixture is hot in the center. (Exact cooking time depends on the size and shape of the casserole. Use an instant-read thermometer to check the temperature in the center. It should be at least 140°F.)

11. Have a cooling rack ready. Let the timbale cool on the rack 10 minutes. Run a knife or a metal spatula around the inside edge of the casserole dish. Place a large platter over the casserole. Holding the dish (with a pot holder) firmly against the platter, invert both to transfer the timbale onto the platter. Sprinkle with parsley. Cut into wedges to serve. Serve hot.

Rice and Beans, Veneto Style

Riso e Fagioli alla Veneta

Makes 4 servings

During the summer, rice and beans are served warm, not hot. In the Veneto region, cranberry beans, known in Italian as borlotti, *are the favorite variety. Uncooked cranberry beans are pink with cream-colored markings. When cooked they turn a solid pinkish beige. They look a lot like pinto beans, which can be substituted if you prefer them.*

About 2 cups homemade <u>Meat Broth</u> or store-bought beef broth

3 tablespoons oil

1 small onion, finely chopped

1 medium carrot, finely chopped

1 medium celery rib, finely chopped

½ cup finely chopped pancetta

2 cups cooked dried cranberry or pinto beans, or 1 (16-ounce) can beans with their liquid

1 cup medium-grain rice, such as Arborio, Carnaroli, or Vialone Nano

Salt and freshly ground black pepper

1. Prepare the broth, if necessary. Then, in a wide heavy saucepan over medium heat, heat the oil with the onion, carrot, celery, and pancetta. Cook, stirring occasionally, until the vegetables are golden, about 20 minutes.

2. Add the beans and 1 cup cold water. Bring to a simmer and cook 20 minutes.

3. Set aside about one-third of the bean mixture. Puree the remainder in a food processor or food mill until smooth. Pour the bean puree and 1 cup of the broth into a large wide saucepan. Bring to a simmer over medium heat. Cook, stirring occasionally, for 5 minutes.

4. Add the rice to the pan, and salt and pepper to taste. Cook 20 minutes, stirring frequently so that the beans do not stick to the bottom of the pan. Add some of the remaining broth a little at a time, until the rice is tender yet still firm. Stir in the reserved bean mixture and turn off the heat.

5. Let rest 5 minutes. Serve hot.

Sardinian Sausage Rice

Riso alla Sarda

Makes 6 servings

More like a pilaf than a risotto, this traditional rice dish from Sardinia does not require a lot of stirring.

About 3 cups <u>Meat Broth</u>

1 medium onion, chopped

2 tablespoons chopped fresh flat-leaf parsley

2 tablespoons olive oil

12 ounces plain Italian pork sausage, casings removed

1 cup peeled, seeded, and chopped tomatoes

Salt and freshly ground black pepper

1½ cups medium-grain rice, such as Arborio, Carnaroli, or Vialone Nano

½ cup freshly grated Pecorino Romano or Parmigiano-Reggiano

1. Prepare the broth, if necessary. Then, in a wide heavy saucepan over medium heat, cook the onion and parsley in the oil until the onion is softened, about 5 minutes. Add the sausage meat and cook, stirring often, until the sausage is lightly browned, about 15 minutes.

2. Stir in the tomatoes and salt and pepper to taste. Add the broth and bring it to a simmer. Stir in the rice. Cover and cook 10 minutes. Check to see if the mixture is too dry. Add more broth or water if needed. Cover and cook 8 minutes more or until the rice is tender.

3. Remove the pan from the heat. Stir in the cheese. Serve immediately.

Polenta

Makes 4 servings

The traditional way of cooking polenta is to pour the dry cornmeal slowly in a fine stream through the fingers of one hand into a pot of boiling water as you stir it constantly with the other hand. You need a lot of patience to do this correctly; if you go too fast, the cornmeal will form lumps. Meanwhile, your hand is burning from being held over the simmering liquid.

I much prefer the method below for cooking polenta because it is quick and foolproof. Best of all, I have tried this method side by side with the traditional method, and I cannot detect any difference in the end result. Because the cornmeal is first mixed with cold water, lumps, which can easily occur if the dry meal is poured directly into the hot water, do not form.

Be sure to use a pot with a heavy bottom or the polenta may scorch. You can also place the pot on a Flametamer—a metal disk that fits over a stove burner for added pot insulation to control the heat. (Look for it in kitchenware shops.)

You can vary basic polenta by cooking it with broth or using milk in place of some of the water. Stir in some grated cheese at the end of the cooking time, if you wish.

4 cups cold water

1 cup coarsely ground yellow cornmeal, preferably stone-ground

2 teaspoons salt

2 tablespoons unsalted butter

1. In a 2-quart heavy saucepan, bring 3 cups water to a boil.

2. Meanwhile, in a small bowl, whisk together the cornmeal, salt, and remaining 1 cup water.

3. Pour the mixture into the boiling water and cook, stirring, until the mixture comes to a boil. Reduce the heat to low, cover, and cook, stirring occasionally, until the polenta is thick and creamy, about 30 minutes. If the polenta becomes too thick, stir in a little more water.

4. Stir in the butter. Serve immediately.

Polenta with Cream

Polenta alla Panna

Makes 4 servings

On a cold winter day in Milan, I stopped for lunch at a busy trattoria. The menu was limited, but this simple, comforting dish was the day's special. If you have a fresh white or black truffle, shave it over the mascarpone and eliminate the cheese.

To warm a serving bowl or platter, place it in a warm (not hot!) oven for a few minutes or run hot water over it in the sink. Dry the bowl or platter before adding the food.

1 recipe (about 5 cups) hot cooked <u>Polenta</u>

1 cup mascarpone or heavy cream

Chunk of Parmigiano-Reggiano

1. Prepare the polenta, if necessary. Then pour the hot cooked polenta onto a warm serving platter.

2. Spoon the mascarpone on top or pour on the cream. With a swivel-blade vegetable peeler, shave the Parmigiano over the top. Serve immediately.

Polenta with Ragù

Polenta al Ragù

Makes 4 servings

At one time many northern Italian families had a special copper pot called a paiolo, *in which they cooked polenta, and a round board on which they served it. This is delicious comfort food, and quite simple if you have the ragù and the polenta made in advance.*

1 recipe (about 3 cups) Ragù Bolognese

1 recipe (about 5 cups) hot cooked Polenta

½ cup freshly grated Parmigiano-Reggiano

1. Prepare the ragù and the polenta, if necessary.

2. Pour the polenta onto a warm platter. Make a shallow indentation in the polenta. Spoon on the sauce. Sprinkle with the cheese and serve immediately.

Polenta Crostini, Three Ways

Slices of crisped polenta can be used in place of bread to make Crostini). Serve them with a tasty topping (see suggestions that follow) as appetizers, as a side dish with a stew, or as a base for grilled or roasted birds.

1 recipe (about 5 cups) hot cooked Polenta

1. **Prepare the polenta.** As soon as the polenta is cooked, spread it with a rubber spatula to about $1/2$-inch thickness on a large baking sheet. Cover and chill until firm, at least 1 hour and up to 3 days, before using.

2. When ready to cook, cut the polenta into squares or another shape with a knife, or cookie or biscuit cutter. The pieces can be baked, broiled, grilled, or fried.

Baked Polenta Crostini: Preheat the oven to 400°F. Oil a baking sheet and arrange the polenta slices on the sheet about $1/2$ inch apart. Brush the tops with oil. Bake 30 minutes or until crisp and lightly golden.

Grilled or Broiled Polenta Crostini: Place a barbecue grill or broiler rack about 4 inches away from the heat source. Preheat the grill or broiler. Brush the polenta slices on both sides with olive oil. Place the pieces on the rack. Grill or broil, turning once, until crisp and golden, about 5 minutes. Turn the pieces and grill the other side about 5 minutes more.

Fried Polenta Crostini: Very lightly brush a thin film of corn or olive oil in a nonstick skillet. Heat the skillet over medium heat. Pat the polenta pieces dry. Cook them until golden, about 5 minutes. Turn the pieces and cook until browned on the other side, about 5 minutes more.

Polenta Sandwiches

Panini di Polenta

Makes 8 servings

These little sandwiches can be served as appetizers or as a side dish. For a little flair, cut out the polenta with cookie or biscuit cutters.

1 recipe (about 5 cups) Polenta, made without butter

4 ounces gorgonzola, thinly sliced

2 tablespoons melted unsalted butter

2 tablespoons Parmigiano-Reggiano

1. Prepare the polenta. As soon as the polenta is cooked, spread it with a rubber spatula to about a $1/2$-inch thickness on a large baking sheet. Cover and chill until firm, at least 1 hour and up to 3 days, before using.

2. Place a rack in the center of the oven. Preheat the oven to 400°F. Butter a large baking sheet.

3. Cut the polenta into 16 squares. Place half the polenta slices on the cookie sheet. Place the gorgonzola slices on top of them. Top

with the remaining polenta, pressing down lightly on the sandwiches.

4. Brush the tops with the butter. Sprinkle with the Parmigiano. Bake 10 to 15 minutes or until the cheese is just melted. Serve hot.

Polenta with Three Cheeses

Polenta con Tre Formaggi

Makes 4 servings

The Valle d'Aosta is the region in the far northwestern corner of Italy. It is famed for its Alpine climate and beautiful ski resorts, as well as dairy products, such as Fontina Valle d'Aosta, a semifirm cows' milk cheese.

Milk adds extra richness to this polenta. Butter stands in as an honorary cheese.

2 cups cold water

1 cup coarsely ground yellow cornmeal, preferably stone-ground

1 teaspoon salt

2 cups cold milk

½ cup Fontina Valle d'Aosta, chopped

¼ cup freshly grated Parmigiano-Reggiano

2 tablespoons unsalted butter

1. In a 2-quart heavy saucepan, bring the water to a boil.

2. In a small bowl, whisk together the cornmeal, salt, and milk.

3. Pour the cornmeal mixture into the boiling water and cook, stirring, until the mixture comes to a boil. Reduce the heat to low, cover, and cook, stirring occasionally, about 30 minutes or until the polenta is thick and creamy. If the polenta becomes too thick, stir in a little more water.

4. Remove the pan from the heat. Stir in the cheeses and butter until melted. Serve immediately.

Polenta with Gorgonzola and Mascarpone

Makes 4 to 6 servings

Heavenly and rich, this recipe is from Lombardy, where gorgonzola and mascarpone are made.

4 cups cold water

1 cup coarsely ground yellow cornmeal, preferably stone-ground

½ teaspoon salt

½ cup mascarpone

½ cup gorgonzola, crumbled

1. In a 2-quart heavy saucepan, bring 3 cups water to a boil.

2. In a small bowl, whisk together the cornmeal, salt, and remaining 1 cup of water.

3. Pour the cornmeal mixture into the boiling water and cook, stirring constantly, until the mixture comes to a boil. Reduce the heat to low, cover, and cook, stirring occasionally, about 30 minutes or until the polenta is thick and creamy. If the polenta becomes too thick, stir in a little more water.

4. Remove the polenta from the heat. Stir in the mascarpone and half of the gorgonzola. Pour into a serving bowl and sprinkle with the remaining gorgonzola. Serve hot.

Mushroom Polenta

Polenta con Funghi

Makes 6 servings

Pancetta adds rich flavor, but leave it out if you prefer a meatless dish. Leftovers can be cut into slices and fried in a little olive oil or butter as an appetizer or side dish.

2 ounces finely chopped pancetta

1 small onion, finely chopped

2 tablespoons olive oil

1 (10-ounce) package white mushrooms, trimmed and sliced

2 tablespoons chopped fresh flat-leaf parsley

Salt and freshly ground black pepper

4 cups cold water

1 cup coarsely ground yellow cornmeal, preferably stone-ground

1. In a large skillet, combine the pancetta, the onion, and the oil and cook until the pancetta and onion are lightly golden, about

10 minutes. Add the mushrooms and parsley and cook until the mushroom liquid evaporates, about 10 minutes more. Season to taste with salt and pepper.

2. In a 2-quart heavy saucepan, bring 3 cups water to a boil.

3. In a small bowl, whisk together the cornmeal, $1/2$ teaspoon salt, and remaining 1 cup cold water.

4. Pour the cornmeal mixture into the boiling water and cook, stirring constantly, until it comes to a boil. Reduce the heat to very low, cover, and cook, stirring occasionally, until the polenta is thick and creamy, about 30 minutes. If the polenta becomes too thick, stir in more water.

5. Stir the contents of the skillet into the polenta saucepan. Pour the mixture onto a warm platter. Serve immediately.

Buckwheat and Cornmeal Polenta

Polenta Taragna

Makes 4 to 6 servings

In Lombardy, this hearty polenta is made with a combination of cornmeal and buckwheat flour. The buckwheat adds an earthy flavor. A local cheese known as bitto *is stirred in at the end of the cooking time. I have never seen* bitto *in the United States, but fontina and Gruyère are good substitutes.*

5 cups cold water

4 tablespoons unsalted butter

1 cup coarsely ground yellow cornmeal, preferably stone-ground

½ cup buckwheat flour

Salt

4 ounces fontina or Gruyère

1. In a 2-quart heavy saucepan, bring 4 cups of the water and 2 tablespoons of the butter to a boil.

2. In a medium bowl, stir together the cornmeal, buckwheat flour, $1/2$ teaspoon salt, and remaining 1 cup water.

3. Whisk the cornmeal mixture into the boiling water. Reduce the heat to very low. Cover and cook, stirring occasionally, about 40 minutes or until the polenta is thick and creamy. If it gets too thick, add a little more water as needed.

4. Remove the polenta from the heat. Stir in the remaining 2 tablespoons butter and the cheese. Serve immediately.

Baked Polenta with Cheese

Polenta Cunsa

Makes 8 servings

Assemble up to 24 hours before cooking but, if it is chilled, double the cooking time. Also try it with Gruyère or Asiago.

5 cups cold water

1 cup coarsely ground yellow cornmeal, preferably stone-ground

1 teaspoon salt

3 tablespoons unsalted butter

1 medium onion, chopped

1 cup freshly grated Parmigiano-Reggiano

½ cup crumbled gorgonzola

½ cup shredded Fontina Valle d'Aosta

1. In a 2-quart heavy saucepan, bring 4 cups water to a boil. In a bowl, whisk together the cornmeal, salt, and the remaining 1 cup water.

2. Pour the mixture into the boiling water and cook, stirring constantly, until the mixture comes to a boil. Reduce the heat to low, cover, and cook, stirring occasionally, about 30 minutes or until the polenta is thick and creamy. If the polenta becomes too thick, stir in a little more water.

3. In a small skillet, melt 2 tablespoons of the butter over medium heat. Add the onion and cook, stirring, until the onion is tender and golden, about 10 minutes. Scrape the onion into the polenta.

4. Place a rack in the center of the oven. Preheat the oven to 375°F. Butter a 9 × 3-inch baking pan.

5. Pour about one third of the polenta into the pan. Set aside $1/4$ cup of the Parmigiano for the topping. Scatter half of each of the remaining cheeses onto the polenta layer in the pan. Make a second layer of polenta and the cheese. Pour on the remaining polenta and spread it evenly.

6. Sprinkle the reserved $1/4$ cup of Parmigiano over the polenta. Dot with the remaining butter. Bake 30 minutes or until bubbling around the edge. Let rest 10 minutes before serving.

Baked Polenta with Sausage Ragù

Polenta Pasticciato

Makes 6 servings

This is something like lasagne, with layers of sliced polenta replacing the pasta.

The name polenta pasticciato *is intriguing. It comes from* pasticciare, *meaning to make a mess of something, but* pasticciato *also indicates a dish made like pasta, with cheese and ragù.*

>1 recipe <u>Sausage Ragù</u>

8 cups cold water

2 cups coarsely ground yellow cornmeal, preferably stone-ground

1 tablespoon salt

8 ounces fresh mozzarella

½ cup freshly grated Parmigiano-Reggiano

1. Prepare the ragù, if necessary. In a large saucepan, bring 6 cups of the water to a boil.

2. In a medium bowl, stir together the cornmeal, salt, and remaining 2 cups of water.

3. Pour the cornmeal mixture into the boiling water, stirring constantly, until the mixture comes to a boil. Reduce the heat to low, cover, and cook, stirring occasionally, about 30 minutes or until the polenta is thick and creamy.

4. Butter a large baking sheet. Pour the polenta into the pan and spread it evenly with a rubber spatula to a $1/2$-inch thickness. Let cool until firm, about least 1 hour, or cover and refrigerate overnight.

5. Place a rack in the center of the oven. Preheat the oven to 400°F. Oil a 9-inch square baking dish.

6. Cut the polenta into 9 3-inch squares. Arrange half the polenta in the bottom of the dish. Spoon on half the sauce and top with half the mozzarella and Parmigiano-Reggiano. Make a second layer of the remaining ingredients.

7. Bake 40 minutes or until the polenta is bubbling and the cheese is melted. Let stand 10 minutes before serving.

Polenta "in Chains"

Polenta Incatenata

Makes 6 servings

My husband and I once rented an apartment in a villa outside of Lucca in Tuscany. Carlotta was the cheerful housekeeper who took care of the place and kept everything running smoothly. Once in a while, she would surprise us with a home-cooked meal. She told me that this hearty polenta, a local specialty, is said to be "chained" in ribbons of shredded vegetables. Serve this as a vegetarian main dish or a side dish with grilled meat. It is also very good if allowed to cool until it solidifies, then sliced and fried until golden brown.

2 tablespoons olive oil

1 garlic clove, finely chopped

2 cups shredded cabbage or kale

4 cups cold water

1 cup coarsely ground yellow cornmeal, preferably stone-ground

1½ teaspoons salt

2 cups cooked or canned cannelini beans

Salt and freshly ground black pepper

½ cup freshly grated Parmigiano-Reggiano

1. In a large saucepan, cook the oil and garlic over medium heat until the garlic is golden, about 2 minutes. Add the cabbage, cover, and cook 10 minutes or until the cabbage is wilted.

2. Add 3 cups of the water and bring it to a simmer.

3. In a small bowl, stir together the cornmeal, salt, and remaining 1 cup of water.

4. Pour the cornmeal mixture into the saucepan. Cook, stirring frequently, until the mixture comes to a simmer. Reduce the heat to low, cover, and cook, stirring occasionally, 20 minutes.

5. Stir in the beans. Cook 10 minutes more or until thick and creamy. Add a little water if the mixture becomes too thick.

6. Remove from the heat. Stir in the cheese and serve immediately.

Farro Salad

Insalata di Farro

Makes 6 servings

In Abruzzo, my husband and I had farro salads on several occasions, including this one with crunchy bits of vegetables and refreshing mint.

Salt

1½ cups farro

1 cup finely chopped carrots

1 cup finely chopped celery

2 tablespoons finely chopped fresh mint

2 green onions, finely chopped

⅓ cup olive oil

1 tablespoon fresh lemon juice

Freshly ground black pepper

1. Bring 6 cups of water to a boil. Add salt to taste, then the farro. Reduce the heat to a simmer and cook until the farro is tender yet still chewy, about 15 to 30 minutes. (Cooking time can vary; start tasting after 15 minutes.) Drain well.

2. In a large bowl, combine the farro, carrots, celery, and mint. In a small bowl, mix together the olive oil, lemon juice, and pepper. Pour the dressing over the salad and toss well. Taste and adjust seasoning. Serve warm or at room temperature.

Farro, Amatrice Style

Farro all'Amatriciana

Makes 8 servings

Farro is usually used in soups or salads, but in this recipe from the Roman countryside, the grain is simmered with a classic Amatriciana sauce, typically used on pasta.

Salt

2 cups farro

¼ cup olive oil

4 ounces pancetta, chopped

1 medium onion

½ cup dry white wine

1½ cups peeled, seeded, and chopped fresh tomatoes, or drained and chopped canned tomatoes

½ cup freshly grated Pecorino Romano

1. Bring 6 cups of water to a boil. Add salt to taste, then the farro. Reduce the heat to a simmer and cook until the farro is tender,

yet still chewy, 15 to 30 minutes. (Cooking time can vary; start tasting after 15 minutes.) Drain well.

2. In a medium skillet, cook the oil, pancetta, and onion over medium heat, stirring often, until the onion is golden, about 10 minutes. Add the wine and bring to a simmer. Add the tomatoes and farro. Bring to a simmer and cook until the farro has absorbed some of the sauce, about 10 minutes. Add a little water if needed to prevent sticking.

3. Remove from the heat. Add the cheese and stir well. Serve immediately.

Farro, Tomatoes, and Cheese

Grano, Pomodori, e Cacio

Makes 6 servings

Wheat berries, emmer, kamut, or other similar grains can be cooked this way if you cannot find farro. Don't add too much salt to the grain, as the ricotta salata can be salty. If it is not available, substitute Pecorino Romano. This recipe is from Puglia in the south.

Salt

1½ cups farro

2 tablespoons olive oil

1 small onion, finely chopped

8 ounces chopped tomatoes

4 ounces ricotta salata, coarsely grated

1. Bring 6 cups of water to a boil. Add salt to taste, then the farro. Reduce the heat to a simmer and cook until the farro is tender, 15 to 30 minutes. (Cooking time can vary; start tasting after 15 minutes.) Drain well.

2. Pour the oil into a medium saucepan. Add the onion and cook, stirring frequently, until the onion is golden, about 10 minutes. Add the tomatoes and salt to taste. Cook until slightly thickened, about 10 minutes.

3. Stir the drained farro into the tomato sauce. Add the cheese and stir well. Serve hot.

Shrimp and Barley Orzotto

Orzotto di Gamberi

Makes 4 servings

Though most people in the United States think of orzo as a tiny seed-shape pasta, in Italian orzo *means "barley." In Friuli–Venezia Giulia in the north, barley is cooked like risotto, and the finished dish is called orzotto.*

3 cups <u>Chicken Broth</u>, vegetable broth, or water

2 tablespoons unsalted butter

1 tablespoon olive oil

1 small onion, finely chopped

1 small carrot, finely chopped

½ cup finely chopped celery

1 garlic clove, minced

6 ounces (⅔ cup) pearl barley, rinsed and drained

Salt and freshly ground black pepper

8 ounces shrimp, shelled and deveined

2 tablespoons chopped fresh flat-leaf parsley

1. Prepare the broth, if necessary. In a medium saucepan, melt the butter with the oil over medium heat. Add the onion, carrot, celery, and garlic and cook until golden, about 10 minutes.

2. Add the barley to the vegetables in the skillet and stir well. Add the broth, 1 teaspoon salt, and pepper to taste. Bring to a simmer and reduce the heat. Cover and cook, stirring occasionally, 30 to 40 minutes or until the barley is tender. Add a little water if the mixture becomes dry.

3. Meanwhile, chop the shrimp and stir them and the parsley into the barley mixture. Cook until the shrimp are just pink, 2 to 3 minutes. Taste and adjust seasoning. Serve immediately.

Barley and Vegetable Orzotto

Orzotto di Verdure

Makes 4 servings

Tiny bits of vegetables are cooked with barley for this orzotto. Serve it as a side dish or first course.

4 cups Meat Broth or Chicken Broth

4 tablespoons unsalted butter

1 small onion, finely chopped

1 cup pearl barley, rinsed and drained

½ cup fresh or frozen peas

½ cup chopped mushrooms, any kind

¼ cup finely chopped red bell pepper

¼ cup finely chopped celery

Salt and freshly ground black pepper

¼ cup freshly grated Parmigiano-Reggiano

1. Prepare the broth, if necessary. In a large saucepan, melt 3 tablespoons of the butter over medium heat. Add the onion and cook, stirring frequently, until golden, about 10 minutes.

2. Add the barley and stir well. Stir in half each of the peas, mushrooms, bell pepper, and celery and cook 2 minutes or until wilted. Add the broth and bring to a simmer. Cover and cook 20 minutes.

3. Stir in the remaining vegetables and salt and pepper to taste. Cook, uncovered, 10 minutes more or until the liquid has evaporated and the barley is tender. Remove from the heat.

4. Stir in the remaining tablespoon of butter and the cheese. Serve immediately.

Prosciutto and Eggs

Uova al Prosciutto

Makes 2 servings

A friend with whom I was traveling in Italy was on a high protein diet. She got into the habit of ordering a plate of prosciutto for breakfast. At one little inn in Montepulciano in Tuscany, the host asked if she would like to have some eggs with the prosciutto. My friend said yes, expecting to get a couple of boiled eggs. Instead, a short time later out came the cook with an individual frying pan filled with sizzling prosciutto and sunny-side-up eggs. It looked and smelled so good, soon everyone in the dining room was ordering the same thing, much to the dismay of the harried cook.

This is a perfect way to use up prosciutto that has gotten a little dry around the edges. Serve eggs with prosciutto for brunch with buttered asparagus and roasted tomatoes.

1 tablespoon unsalted butter

4 to 6 thin slices imported Italian prosciutto

4 large eggs

Salt and freshly ground black pepper

1. In a 9-inch nonstick skillet, melt the butter over medium-low heat.

2. Lay the prosciutto slices in the pan, overlapping slightly. Break the eggs into a cup one at a time, then slide the eggs onto the prosciutto. Sprinkle with salt and pepper.

3. Cover and cook over low heat until the eggs are set to taste, about 2 to 3 minutes. Serve hot.

Baked Asparagus with Eggs

Asparagi Milanese

Makes 2 to 4 servings

A journalist once asked me what I eat for dinner when I am cooking for myself. Without giving it much thought I replied asparagus with eggs and Parmigiano—what the Italians call Milanese style. This is so good, yet so simple. It is my idea of comfort food.

1 pound asparagus

Salt

3 tablespoons unsalted butter

Freshly ground black pepper

½ cup freshly grated Parmigiano-Reggiano

4 large eggs

1. **Trim off the base of the asparagus at the point where the stem turns from white to green. Bring about 2 inches of water to a boil in a large skillet. Add the asparagus and salt to taste. Cook until the asparagus bend slightly when you lift them from the stem end, about 4 to 8 minutes. Cooking time will depend on the

thickness of the asparagus. Transfer the asparagus with tongs to a strainer. Drain, then pat them dry.

2. Place a rack in the center of the oven. Preheat the oven to 450°F. Butter a large baking dish.

3. Arrange the asparagus side by side in the baking dish, overlapping them slightly. Dot with 1 tablespoon of the butter, and sprinkle with pepper and the cheese.

4. Bake 15 minutes or until the cheese is melted and golden.

5. In a large nonstick skillet, melt the remaining 2 tablespoons butter over medium heat. When the butter foam subsides, break one egg into a cup, then carefully slide it into the pan. Repeat with the remaining eggs. Sprinkle with salt and cook until the eggs are set to taste, about 2 to 3 minutes.

6. Divide the asparagus among the plates. Place the eggs on top. Spoon the pan juices over the top and serve hot.

Eggs in Purgatory

Uova in Purgatorio

Makes 4 servings

When I was growing up, Friday night dinner at our house was always a meatless meal. Our meals were based on Neapolitan cooking. Dinner usually consisted of pasta e fagioli *(pasta and beans)*, tuna salad, or these delicious eggs cooked in a spicy tomato sauce, hence the charming name Eggs in Purgatory. This is a perfect dish for when there is not much in the pantry and you want something hot and quick. Crusty bread is the essential accompaniment.

2 tablespoons olive oil

¼ cup finely chopped onion

2 cups canned peeled tomatoes, chopped

4 fresh basil leaves, torn into pieces, or a pinch of dried oregano

Pinch of crushed red pepper (*peperoncino*)

Salt

8 large eggs

1. Pour the oil into a medium skillet. Add the onion and cook over medium heat, stirring, until tender and golden, about 10 minutes. Add the tomatoes, basil, red pepper, and salt to taste. Bring to a simmer and cook 15 minutes or until thickened.

2. Break an egg into a small cup. With a spoon, make an indentation in the tomato sauce. Slide the egg into the sauce. Continue with the remaining eggs.

3. Cover the skillet and cook until the eggs are set to taste, 2 to 3 minutes. Serve hot.

Eggs in Tomato Sauce, Marches Style

Uova in Brodetto

Makes 2 servings

My uncle Joe, whose family came from the Marche region on the eastern coast of Italy, had a special way of cooking eggs in tomato sauce. His recipe, though similar to <u>Eggs in Purgatory</u>, contains a dash of vinegar for a tangy flavor.

1 small onion, very finely chopped

1 tablespoon fresh flat-leaf parsley, very finely chopped

2 tablespoons olive oil

1½ cups peeled, seeded, and chopped fresh tomatoes or drained and chopped canned tomatoes

1 to 2 tablespoons white wine vinegar

Salt and freshly ground black pepper

4 large eggs

1. In a 9-inch nonstick skillet, combine the onion, parsley, and oil and cook over medium heat, stirring occasionally, until the onion is tender and golden, about 10 minutes.

2. Stir in the tomatoes, vinegar, salt, and pepper to taste. Cook 10 minutes or until the sauce is thickened.

3. Break an egg into a small cup. With a spoon, make an indentation in the sauce. Carefully drop in the egg. Repeat with the remaining eggs. Sprinkle with salt and pepper. Cover and cook until the eggs are set to taste, 2 to 3 minutes. Serve hot.

Piedmontese-Style Eggs

Uova al Cirighet

Makes 4 servings

Numerous dishes in Piedmont are flavored with garlic and anchovies sharpened with vinegar. Here, eggs get this piquant, flavorful treatment.

4 tablespoons olive oil

4 anchovy fillets, drained and chopped

2 tablespoons chopped fresh flat-leaf parsley

2 tablespoons capers, rinsed and drained

2 garlic cloves, very finely chopped

2 sage leaves, chopped

Pinch of crushed red pepper

1 tablespoon red wine vinegar

1 to 2 teaspoons fresh lemon juice

2 tablespoons unsalted butter

8 large eggs

Salt

1. In a medium skillet, combine the oil, anchovies, parsley, capers, garlic, sage, and crushed red pepper. Cook over medium heat, stirring often, until the anchovies are dissolved, 4 to 5 minutes. Stir in the vinegar and lemon juice. Cook 1 minute more.

2. In a large nonstick skillet, melt the butter over medium heat. When the butter foam subsides, carefully slide the eggs into the pan. Sprinkle with salt and cook 2 to 3 minutes, or until the eggs are set to taste.

3. Spoon the sauce over the eggs. Serve immediately.

Eggs Florentine

Uova alla Fiorentina

Makes 4 servings

Eggs Florentine is often made in the United States with butter and a rich hollandaise sauce. This is a version that I had in Florence. Instead of butter, the spinach is cooked with garlic and olive oil, and a light sprinkling of Parmigiano is all that is needed on top of the eggs. It is a much lighter preparation, perfect for a casual brunch.

3 pounds spinach, tough stems removed

Salt

2 tablespoons olive oil

1 garlic clove, finely chopped

Freshly ground black pepper

8 eggs

2 tablespoons freshly grated Parmigiano-Reggiano

1. Wash the spinach well in several changes of cold water. Put the spinach, $1/2$ cup water, and a pinch of salt into a large pot. Cover the pot and turn on the heat to medium. Cook 5 minutes or until the spinach is wilted and tender. Drain the spinach and press out the excess water.

2. Pour the oil into a large skillet. Add the garlic and cook until golden, about 2 minutes.

3. Stir in the spinach and salt and pepper to taste. Cook, stirring occasionally, until heated through, about 2 minutes.

4. Break an egg into a small cup. With a spoon, make an indentation in the spinach. Slide the egg into the indentation. Repeat with the remaining eggs.

5. Sprinkle the eggs with salt and pepper and the cheese. Cover the skillet and cook 2 to 3 minutes or until the eggs are set to taste. Serve hot.

Baked Eggs with Potatoes and Cheese

Uova al Forno

Makes 4 servings

Neapolitan comfort food is the best way to describe this layered casserole of potatoes, cheese, and eggs that my mother often made for me when I was a child.

1 pound all-purpose potatoes, such as Yukon gold

Salt

1 tablespoon unsalted butter

8 ounces fresh mozzarella, sliced

4 large eggs

Freshly ground black pepper

2 tablespoons Parmigiano-Reggiano

1. Scrub the potatoes and peel them. Cut them into $1/4$-inch-thick slices. Place the potatoes in a medium saucepan with cold water to cover and salt to taste. Cover and bring to a simmer. Cook until the potatoes are just tender when pierced with a fork, about 10 minutes. Drain the potatoes and cool slightly.

2. Place a rack in the center of the oven. Preheat the oven to 400°F. Smear the butter around the bottom and sides of a 9-inch square baking dish. Arrange the potato slices in the pan, overlapping them slightly. Place the cheese slices on top of the potatoes. Break the eggs into a small cup, then slide them into the pan on top of the cheese. Sprinkle with salt, pepper, and the grated Parmigiano-Reggiano.

3. Bake until the eggs are set to taste, about 15 minutes. Serve hot.

Peppers and Eggs

Peperoni e le Uova

Makes 4 servings

Sautéed peppers or potatoes finished with scrambled eggs are good for brunch with grilled sausages, or serve them stuffed into wedges of crisp Italian bread for classic hero sandwiches.

¼ cup olive oil

2 medium red bell peppers, cut into bite-size pieces

1 medium green bell pepper, cut into bite-size pieces

1 small onion, thinly sliced

Salt

8 large eggs

¼ cup freshly grated Parmigiano-Reggiano

Freshly ground black pepper

1. In a 9-inch nonstick skillet, heat the oil over medium heat. Add the peppers, onion, and salt to taste. Cook, stirring often, until the peppers are browned, about 20 minutes. Cover and cook 5 minutes more or until the peppers are very tender.

2. In a medium bowl, beat the eggs with the cheese and add salt and ground pepper to taste. Pour the eggs over the peppers and let them set briefly. Turn the peppers and eggs with a spatula or spoon to allow the uncooked eggs to reach the surface of the pan. Allow the eggs to set and stir again. Repeat the stirring and cooking until the eggs are set to taste, about 2 to 3 minutes. Serve hot.

Potatoes and Eggs

Patate con le Uuova

Makes 4 servings

Potatoes scrambled with eggs is a classic combination found all over southern Italy. A small, thinly sliced bell pepper or an onion—or both—can be fried along with the potatoes, if you like. Serve it with sausages for brunch or stuff the potatoes and eggs into Italian bread for a hero sandwich.

¼ cup olive oil

4 waxy new potatoes, peeled and cut into ¼-inch slices

Salt

8 large eggs

Freshly ground black pepper

1. In a 9-inch nonstick skillet, heat the oil over medium heat. Pat the potato slices dry, and place them in the skillet. Cook, turning the pieces frequently, until the potatoes are browned and tender, about 10 minutes. Sprinkle with salt.

2. In a medium bowl, beat the eggs with salt and pepper to taste. Pour the eggs into the pan and let them set briefly. Turn the potatoes and eggs with a spatula or spoon to allow the uncooked eggs to reach the surface of the pan. Allow the eggs to set and stir again. Repeat the stirring and cooking until the eggs are set to taste, about 2 to 3 minutes. Serve hot.

Mushroom and Egg Scramble

Uova con Funghi

Makes 4 servings

Eggs scrambled with mushrooms are good for a light supper or brunch. White mushrooms are fine, but wild mushrooms add a great earthy flavor.

3 tablespoons unsalted butter

1 small onion, finely chopped

2 cups sliced mushrooms

Salt and freshly ground black pepper

8 large eggs

1. In a 9-inch nonstick skillet, melt the butter over medium heat. Add the onion, mushrooms, and salt and pepper to taste. Cook, stirring occasionally, until the mushrooms are lightly browned, about 10 minutes.

2. In a medium bowl, beat the eggs with salt and pepper to taste. Pour the eggs over the vegetables and let them set briefly. Turn

the mushrooms and eggs with a spatula or spoon to allow the uncooked eggs to reach the surface of the pan. Allow the eggs to set and stir again. Repeat the stirring and cooking until the eggs are set to taste, about 2 to 3 minutes. Serve hot.

Onion and Arugula Frittata

Frittata di Cipolle e Rughetta

Makes 4 servings

One day, an old friend of my mother's from Palermo in Sicily came to visit. We knew her as Zia Millie, though she was not really an aunt. She offered to prepare a salad to go with our meal and asked me if I had any mild onions, such as the red or white varieties. I only had the yellow onions that I typically use for cooking, but she said it would be fine. She sliced an onion thin and soaked it in several changes of cold water, which removed the powerful juices. By the time we were ready to eat the salad, the onion was as sweet as any milder variety. I use this method often whenever I want a gentle onion flavor.

This frittata from Puglia is flavored with onion and arugula. Substitute watercress or spinach leaves if you have no arugula.

2 medium onions, thinly sliced

3 tablespoons olive oil

1 large bunch of arugula, tough stems removed, torn into bite-size pieces (about 2 cups)

8 large eggs

¼ cup freshly grated Parmigiano-Reggiano

Salt and freshly ground black pepper

1. Place the onions in a bowl with cold water to cover. Let stand 1 hour, changing the water once or twice, until the onions taste sweet. Drain and pat dry.

2. Pour the oil into a 9-inch nonstick skillet. Add the onions. Cook over medium heat, stirring occasionally, until the onions are tender and golden, about 10 minutes. Stir in the arugula until wilted, about 1 minute.

3. 3 In a medium bowl, beat together the eggs, cheese, and salt and pepper to taste. Pour the eggs over the vegetables in the skillet and lower the heat. Cover and cook until the eggs are just set but still moist in the center and the frittata is lightly browned on the bottom, about 5 to 10 minutes.

4. Using a spatula to help, slide the frittata onto a plate. Invert the skillet over the plate and quickly flip both the plate and skillet so that the frittata is back in the pan with the cooked side up. Cook until just set in the center, about 5 minutes more. Or, if you prefer not to flip it, slide the skillet under the broiler 3 to 5 minutes or until the eggs are set to taste.

5. Slide the frittata onto a serving dish and cut into wedges. Serve hot or at room temperature.

Zucchini and Basil Frittata

Frittata di Zucchine

Makes 4 servings

My mother used to grow zucchini in our tiny backyard in Brooklyn. At the height of the season, they grew so quickly we could hardly use them fast enough. That is when my mother would make this simple frittata, which we would eat with a fresh tomato salad. No bigger than a hot dog, the homegrown zucchini were mild and flavorful, with tiny seeds and thin skins.

3 tablespoons olive oil

2 to 3 small zucchini (about 1 pound), scrubbed and sliced

8 large eggs

¼ cup freshly grated Parmigiano-Reggiano

6 fresh basil leaves, stacked and sliced into thin ribbons

Salt and freshly ground black pepper

1. In a 9-inch nonstick skillet, heat the oil over medium-high heat. Add the zucchini and cook, turning the pieces occasionally, until the zucchini are nicely browned, about 12 minutes.

2. In a large bowl, beat the eggs, cheese, basil, and salt and pepper to taste. Lower the heat to medium. Pour the mixture over the zucchini. Lift the edges of the frittata as it sets to allow the uncooked egg to reach the surface of the pan. Cook until the eggs are just set but still moist in the center and the frittata is lightly browned on the bottom, about 5 to 10 minutes.

3. Slide the frittata onto a plate, then invert the skillet over the plate. Quickly flip both the plate and skillet so that the frittata is cooked-side up. Cook until just set in the center, about 5 minutes more. Or, if you prefer not to flip it, slide the skillet under the broiler 3 to 5 minutes or until set to taste. Serve hot or at room temperature.

4. Slide the frittata onto a serving dish and cut into wedges. Serve hot or refrigerate and serve cold.

Hundred-Herb Frittata

Frittata con Cento Erbe

Makes 4 servings

Though I normally use only five or six herbs in this frittata from Friuli–Venezia Giulia, the name implies that the possibilities are much greater, and you can use whatever fresh herbs you have available. Fresh parsley is essential, but if the only other herbs you have on hand are dried, use just a pinch, or their flavors will be overwhelming.

8 large eggs

¼ cup freshly grated Parmigiano-Reggiano

2 tablespoons finely chopped fresh flat-leaf parsley

2 tablespoons finely chopped fresh basil

1 tablespoon chopped fresh chives

1 teaspoon chopped fresh tarragon

1 teaspoon finely chopped fresh thyme

Salt and freshly ground black pepper

2 tablespoons olive oil

1. In a large bowl, beat the eggs, cheese, herbs, and salt and pepper to taste until well combined.

2. In a 9-inch non-stick skillet, heat the oil over medium heat. Pour the egg mixture into the pan. Lift the edges of the frittata as it sets to allow the uncooked egg to reach the surface of the pan. Cook until the eggs are just set but still moist in the center and the frittata is lightly browned on the bottom, about 5 to 10 minutes.

3. Slide the frittata onto a plate, then invert the skillet over the plate. Quickly flip both the plate and skillet so that the frittata is cooked-side up. Cook until just set in the center, about 5 minutes more. Or, if you prefer not to flip it, slide the skillet under the broiler 3 to 5 minutes or until set to taste. Serve hot or at room temperature.

Spinach Frittata

Frittata di Spinaci

Makes 4 servings

Spinach, escarole, Swiss chard, or other greens can be used in this frittata. Serve it with sautéed mushrooms and sliced tomatoes.

1 pound fresh spinach, trimmed

¼ cup water

Salt

8 large eggs

¼ cup heavy cream

½ cup freshly grated Parmigiano-Reggiano

2 tablespoons unsalted butter

1. Place the spinach, water, and salt to taste in a large pot. Cover and cook over medium heat until tender and wilted, about 5 minutes. Drain well. Let cool slightly. Place the spinach in a kitchen towel and squeeze it to extract the liquid.

2. In a large bowl, beat the eggs, cream, cheese, and salt and pepper to taste. Stir in the spinach.

3. In a 9-inch non-stick skillet, melt the butter over medium heat. Pour the mixture into the pan. Lift the edges of the frittata as it sets to allow the uncooked egg to reach the surface of the pan. Cook until the eggs are just set but still moist in the center and the frittata is lightly browned on the bottom, about 5 to 10 minutes.

4. Slide the frittata onto a plate, then invert the skillet over the plate. Quickly flip both the plate and skillet so that the frittata is cooked side up. Cook until set in the center, about 5 minutes more. Or, if you prefer not to flip it, slide the skillet under the broiler for 3 to 5 minutes or until set to taste. Serve hot or at room temperature.

Mushroom and Fontina Frittata

Frittata di Funghi e Fontina

Makes 4 servings

Genuine Fontina Valle d'Aosta has a woodsy, mushroom aroma and marries well with any mushroom dish. Use wild mushrooms if you prefer them to the white.

3 tablespoons unsalted butter

8 ounces mushrooms, halved or quartered if large

Salt and freshly ground black pepper

8 large eggs

2 tablespoons chopped fresh flat-leaf parsley

4 ounces Fontina Valle d'Aosta, cut into slices

1. In a 9-inch non-stick skillet, melt the butter over medium heat. Add the mushrooms and salt and pepper to taste. Cook, stirring often, until the mushrooms are lightly browned, about 10 minutes.

2. In a large bowl, beat the eggs with the parsley and salt and pepper to taste. Lower the heat to medium. Pour the mixture over the mushrooms. Lift the edges of the frittata as it sets to allow the uncooked egg to reach the surface of the pan. Cover and cook until the eggs are just set but still moist in the center and the frittata is lightly browned on the bottom, about 5 to 10 minutes.

3. Place the slices of cheese on top. Slide the skillet under the broiler and cook 1 to 3 minutes or until the cheese has melted and the eggs are set to taste. Or, if you prefer, cover the pan and cook 3 to 5 minutes, until the cheese is melted and the eggs are set to taste.

4. Slide the frittata onto a serving plate. Serve hot.

Neapolitan Spaghetti Frittata

Frittata di Spaghetti

Makes 6 servings

At a family gathering some years ago, a distant relative got to talking about her favorite recipes. She described a flat golden pasta torte filled with meats and cheeses that her children asked for all the time. I wrote down her instructions and tried it at home. It was as good as she said, and I have since learned that it is a traditional Neapolitan recipe. Although you could prepare spaghetti just for this dish, it is traditionally made with leftovers.

8 large eggs

½ cup freshly grated Parmigiano-Reggiano or Pecorino Romano

Salt and freshly ground black pepper

12 ounces spaghetti or other pasta, cooked and drained

4 ounces sliced salami, imported Italian prosciutto, or ham, cut into narrow strips

2 tablespoons olive oil

8 ounces mozzarella, thinly sliced

1. In a large bowl, beat the eggs, cheese, and salt and pepper to taste. Stir in the spaghetti and salami.

2. In a 9-inch nonstick skillet, heat the oil over medium heat. Add half of the spaghetti mixture. Cover with the cheese slices. Pour the remaining pasta mixture over the cheese.

3. Reduce the heat to low. Cook the spaghetti, flattening the surface occasionally, so the pasta sticks together and forms a cake. After about 5 minutes, slide a spatula around the rim of the skillet and lift the cake gently to be sure that it is not sticking. Cook until the eggs are set and the frittata is lightly browned on the bottom, about 15 to 20 minutes.

4. Slide the frittata onto a plate, then invert the skillet over the plate. Quickly flip both the plate and skillet so that the frittata is cooked-side up. Cook until just set in the center, about 5 minutes more. Or, if you prefer not to flip it, slide the skillet under the broiler for 3 to 5 minutes or until set to taste. Serve hot or at room temperature.

Pasta Frittata

Frittata di Pasta

Makes 4 servings

Any leftover pasta can be recycled into this delicious frittata. No matter if the pasta is plain or sauced with tomatoes, meat sauce, or vegetables, this frittata always turns out great. Improvise by adding chopped sausages, ham, cheese, or some cut-up cooked vegetables. Quantities are not really important.

6 large eggs

½ cup freshly grated Parmigiano-Reggiano

Salt and freshly ground black pepper

8 ounces cooked pasta, with or without a sauce

2 tablespoons olive oil

1. In a large bowl, beat together the eggs, cheese, and salt and pepper to taste. Stir in the cooked pasta.

2. In a 9-inch nonstick skillet, heat the oil over medium heat. Add the pasta mixture and press it flat. Cook until the eggs are just

set but still moist in the center and the frittata is lightly browned on the bottom, about 10 minutes.

3. Slide the frittata onto a plate, then invert the skillet over the plate. Quickly flip both the plate and skillet so that the frittata is cooked-side up. Cook until just set in the center, about 5 minutes more. Or, if you prefer not to flip it, slide the skillet under the broiler for 3 to 5 minutes or until set to taste. Serve hot or at room temperature.

Little Omelets

Frittatine

Makes 6 servings

Miniature omelets, prepared on a griddle like pancakes, are nice to serve as part of an antipasto assortment or to use as a sandwich filling. This version made with leeks and cabbage is from Piedmont.

About ¼ cup olive oil

3 cups finely shredded cabbage

1 medium leek, trimmed and thinly sliced

6 large eggs

½ cup freshly grated Parmigiano-Reggiano

½ teaspoon salt

Freshly ground black pepper

1. In a 9-inch nonstick heavy skillet, heat 3 tablespoons oil over medium-low heat. Stir in the cabbage and leek. Cover the skillet and cook, stirring occasionally, until the cabbage is very tender, about 30 minutes. Let cool.

2. In a medium bowl, beat together the eggs, cheese, and salt and pepper to taste. Stir in the vegetable mixture.

3. Lightly brush a griddle or a large nonstick skillet with oil. Heat over medium heat.

4. Stir the egg mixture and scoop by $1/4$ cupful onto the griddle, spacing the omelets about 4 inches apart. Flatten slightly with the back of a spoon. Cook until the eggs are set and the omelets begin to brown on the bottom, about 2 minutes. With a pancake turner, flip the omelets and cook on the other side for about 1 minute more. Transfer the omelets to a plate.

5. Cook the remaining omelets in the same way. Serve hot or at room temperature.

Ricotta and Zucchini Flower Frittata

Frittata di Fiori e Ricotta

Makes 4 servings

Zucchini flowers are not only beautiful but also delicious to eat—something Italians know well. My local farmers' market had an abundance of zucchini flowers one Saturday. I bought some to stuff and fry, but I still had plenty leftover, so I made this frittata with the remaining flowers. It was delicate and delicious; I've made it for brunch several times since.

It can also be made just with ricotta if you don't have zucchini flowers.

2 tablespoons unsalted butter

6 zucchini or other squash blossoms, rinsed and dried

6 large eggs, beaten

¼ cup freshly grated Parmigiano-Reggiano

Salt and freshly ground pepper

1 cup ricotta

1. In a 9-inch nonstick skillet, melt the butter over medium heat. Place the zucchini flowers in the pan in a pinwheel fashion.

2. In a medium bowl, beat together the eggs, Parmigiano, and salt and pepper to taste. Carefully pour the mixture over the flowers without disturbing them. Place spoonfuls of the ricotta around the pan. Lift the edges of the frittata as it sets to allow the uncooked egg to reach the surface of the pan. Cook until the eggs are just set but still moist in the center and the frittata is lightly browned on the bottom, about 5 to 10 minutes.

3. Slide the frittata onto a plate, then invert the skillet over the plate. Quickly flip both the plate and skillet so that the frittata is cooked-side up. Cook until just set in the center, about 5 minutes more. Or, if you prefer not to flip it, slide the skillet under the broiler for 3 to 5 minutes, or until the eggs are set to taste. Serve hot or at room temperature.

Omelet Strips in Tomato Sauce

Fettuccine di Frittata

Makes 4 servings

No pasta? No problem. Make a thin frittata and cut it into strips to resemble fettuccine. Though known as fettuccine di frittata *throughout Italy, in Rome, this dish is called* trippe finte, *meaning false tripe, because the eggs strips resemble innards when cooked this way. Serve it for lunch or dinner with any green vegetable in season, or a green salad.*

> 2 cups <u>Fresh Tomato Sauce</u> or <u>Tuscan Tomato Sauce</u>

8 large eggs

¼ cup freshly grated Parmigiano-Reggiano, plus more for serving

1 tablespoon chopped fresh flat-leaf parsley

1 teaspoon salt

Freshly ground black pepper

2 tablespoons unsalted butter

1. Prepare the tomato sauce, if necessary. Then, place a rack in the center of the oven. Preheat the oven to 400°F. Generously butter a 13 × 9 × 2– inch baking dish.

2. In a medium bowl, beat together the eggs, $1/4$ cup of cheese, parsley, salt, and pepper to taste. Pour the egg mixture into the prepared pan. Bake 8 to 10 minutes or until the eggs are just set and a knife inserted in the center comes out clean.

3. Run a knife around the edge of the pan. Invert the eggs onto a cutting board. Cut the omelet into $1/2$-inch strips.

4. In a 9-inch nonstick skillet, heat the sauce over low heat until simmering. Slip the egg strips into the sauce. Cook, stirring gently, 2 to 3 minutes. Serve hot with grated cheese.

www.ingramcontent.com/pod-product-compliance
Lightning Source LLC
Chambersburg PA
CBHW071819080526
44589CB00012B/851